PROCLAMATION:
Aids for Interpreting the
Lessons of the Church Year

PENTECOST 2

SERIES C

**George W. Hoyer
and
Wolfgang Roth**

FORTRESS PRESS   Philadelphia, Pennsylvania

BV
4241
.P76
Ser.C
Pent.2
c.3

Table of Contents

COPYRIGHT © 1974 by FORTRESS PRESS

All rights reserved. No part of this publication may be reproduced, stored in a retrieval system, or transmitted in any form or by any means, electronic, mechanical, photocopying, recording, or otherwise, without the prior permission of the copyright owner.

Library of Congress Catalog Card Number 73-88347

ISBN 0-8006-4057-8

4060K73   Printed in U.S.A.   1-4057

General Preface

Proclamation: Aids for Interpreting the Lessons of the Church Year is a series of twenty-five books designed to help clergymen carry out their preaching ministry. It offers exegetical interpretations of the lessons for each Sunday and many of the festivals of the church year, plus homiletical ideas and insights.

The basic thrust of the series is ecumenical. In recent years the Episcopal church, the Roman Catholic church, the United Church of Christ, and the Lutheran and Presbyterian churches have adopted lectionaries that are based on a common three-year system of lessons for the Sundays and festivals of the church year. *Proclamation* grows out of this development, and authors have been chosen from all of these traditions. Some of the contributors are parish pastors; others are teachers, both of biblical interpretation and of homiletics. Ecumenical interchange has been encouraged by putting two persons from different traditions to work on a single volume, one with the primary responsibility for exegesis and the other for homiletical interpretation.

Despite the high percentage of agreement between the traditions, both in the festivals that are celebrated and the lessons that are appointed to be read on a given day, there are still areas of divergence. Frequently the authors of individual volumes have tried to take into account the various textual traditions, but in some cases this has proved to be impossible; in such cases we have felt constrained to limit the material to the Lutheran readings.

The preacher who is looking for "canned sermons" in these books will be disappointed. These books are one step removed from the pulpit: they explain what the lessons are saying and suggest ways of relating this biblical message to the contemporary situation. As such they are springboards for creative thought as well as for faithful proclamation of the word.

This volume of *Proclamation* has been prepared by George W. Hoyer, Professor of Practical Theology (Homiletics and Worship) at Concordia Seminary, St. Louis, Mo., and Wolfgang Roth, Professor of Old Testament Interpretation at Garrett Theological Seminary, Evanston, Ill. Prof. Hoyer, the editor-homiletician, is a graduate of Concordia Seminary and a member of the Lutheran Church—Missouri Synod. He has served parishes in Canada and Maryland and has been a professor at Concordia since 1954. Since 1972 he has been dean of the chapel at the seminary. Prof. Roth, the exegete, is a native of Germany and received his basic theological education in that country. He did graduate work in Old Testament and Near Eastern studies in Toronto, Canada, and after the completion of these studies was ordained by the United Church of Canada. He has taught at a theological school in India, served as a parish minister in rural Ontario, and since 1967 has been teaching Old Testament at Garrett Theological Seminary (United Methodist).

The Tenth Sunday after Pentecost

Lutheran	Roman Catholic	Episcopal	Presbyterian and UCC
Gen. 18:20–32	Gen. 18:20–32	Gen. 18:20–32	Gen. 18:20–33
Col. 2:6–15	Col. 2:12–14	Col. 2:6–15	Col. 2:8–15
Luke 11:1–13	Luke 11:1–13	Luke 11:1–13	Luke 11:1–13

EXEGESIS

First Lesson: Gen. 18:20–32. This passage was composed and set within the Sodom-Gomorrah section by the Yahwist as a debate with the Lord on the theme: How just is God's justice? Since Israel is to act justly as instructed by Abraham (18:19), God instructs Abraham and so Israel (18:17–19) as to what "justice" is.

The text seeks to probe the justice of the Lord's action in the violent destruction of the cities near the southern end of the Dead Sea. The Yahwist and his circle in the Solomonic era (10th cent. B.C.) witnessed the disappearance of the tribal-collective social pattern according to which a distinction is not made between guilty and innocent members of a family (cf. Josh. 7:24–25) and the emergence of an urban, real estate based culture where the agonizing question rose: Does the sin of one or several bring disaster over all (cf. for instance, David's murder of Uriah, 2 Samuel 11)? In turn, can the covenantal loyalty of a minority tip the balance toward life for the whole community? Israel was to struggle with this issue time and again, for instance when Ezekiel centuries later affirmed that the true prophet "ventures into the breach" (13:3 ff.; cf. Isa. 53:4–7).

The justice of God as exemplified in the Sodom-Gomorrah story must not be attested by one generation to the next as a divine guarantee that the evil of a community will surely and inescapably ripen into its destruction. Rather, it is a manifestation of covenantal mutuality and loyalty for the good of those covenantally bound together (cf. Gen. 15:6). It is justice that seeks to free the human being so that he may live (Ps. 31:1).

Second Lesson: Col. 2:6–15. The text is the first part of the central section of Colossians (2:6–19) in which Paul (or one of his disciples) develops his Christology in opposition to another christological concept. The highly condensed style in 2:10–15 is due to an excursus-like use of a hymn celebrating the life in Christ. Several already traditional motifs

1

appear, notably the contrast of spiritual circumcision, baptism, with hand-made circumcision, the elimination of all man-made (Jewish or Gentile) laws through the cross, and the triumphal display of principalities and powers taken captive by Christ.

The christological thesis of these verses is that through death, resurrection, and ascension, Christ has overcome all the powers of the realm of the spirits (1:15–2:5) and all the powers of this world, the very powers on which the opponents rely. Christians already share in his victory and fullness through baptism and the ensuing new life (Rom. 6:1–11). Hence, to make the observance or worship of "the elements of the world" (2:8, a philosophically and religiously loaded term, also denoting secretly revealed mystery, mysterious knowledge and, possibly, angelic powers [cf. 2:18]) a condition for moving toward the fullness of Christ is in this Pauline perspective to be rejected as an equivalent of "the law overcome by Christ" (Rom. 10:4).

The opponents of this thesis observe Jewish dietary laws and holy seasons (2:16), worship angelic powers (2:18), and base themselves on "philosophy," rather than on the normative tradition that confesses Jesus as Lord (cf. 1 Cor. 12:3). Hence they must be characterized as a Jewish-Christian Gnostic group, prevalent in the middle of the 1st century A.D. in Asia Minor.

The christological thesis of the writer employs Gnostic patterns, for instance, the triumph of Christ over the powers and the implication that the resurrection of the Christian has already happened (2:12–13; cf. the Gnostic claim in 2 Tim. 2:8). The writer reinterprets these patterns to assert that Christian life is not the esoteric knowledge that opens escape into another realm, but rather the daily mastery of the world in obedience and freedom (2:6–7).

Gospel: Luke 11:1–13. Within the section "Jesus on the way to suffering and ascension" (9:51–18:14), 11:1–13 unfolds the theme: the prayer taught by Jesus to his disciples as pattern of their prayers in "the period of the Holy Spirit," between Jesus' ascension and his appearance in glory (cf. Acts 1:8, 11; 2:1–4).

Luke knows from tradition that a prayer given by a master to his disciples (be he John the Baptist, a rabbi, or Jesus) distinguished this group from the others, that it summarily set forth the central emphasis of the group, and that it became the pattern of prayer for the group. Jesus is introduced (11:1) as one who prays and who teaches what he practices.

Luke 11:2–4 (based on the Q source) gives the Lord's Prayer according to Luke. Luke has five petitions, each exemplified by Jesus' own obedient practice of the request made in the petition (cf. 4:9–12; 4:5–8; 4:2–4;

23:34; 22:39–46). The kingdom of God (cf. Ps. 145:11–13) is understood as the universal but not yet fully recognized reign of God (17:20–21; cf. Rom. 14:17); it is not a spatially conceived realm. Generally the petitions are less apocalyptic than in Matthew; the emphasis is on day by day Christian life.

The parable of the importunate friend at midnight (11:5–8) follows immediately on the Lord's Prayer. Not propriety but need commands prayer. The Palestinian house has one room only; the family sleeps together with doors barred.

The claim that the gift of the Spirit comes in response to prayer (11:9–13; Q source) shows Luke's emphasis: the Holy Spirit is that which makes and marks the Christian community after Pentecost (contrast Matt. 7:11). The command to pray is buttressed in disputation style against those of little faith in prayer, with the familiar Christian and Jewish argument: if you can give good gifts to your children, how much more can God give to you (cf. Matt. 6:30).

HOMILETICAL INTERPRETATION

A theme for the day is *Prayer Is Possible.* A good word in a doubting day! The disciples do not raise contemporary man's question about prayer's possibility; but the word of our Lord is the sharp sword that cuts through to the bone and marrow of the issue and supplies the answer: "When you pray, say: 'Father. . . .' " As dear children we can say, "Father!"

The Judge of all the earth has really done this right (Gen. 18:25)! The primal creation outdone in the incarnation (Gen. 1:27—great creating: making something out of nothing. Phil. 2:7–8—but his incarnating: making nothing out of Something! cf. Ps. 22:6). What makes this supremely *right* for us is that by the incarnation we are brothers of the Son and can join him in saying, "Father!"

The Second Lesson supplies a pertinent pun to warn us lest we be preyed on and cease to be pray-ers (Col. 2:8). Who he is (v. 9) guarantees the possibility of what he urges—"Pray!" Who we are (v. 10) legitimatizes our responding, "Father!"

The Second Lesson warns more sharply of "foes within": "You—dead!" (v. 13). It is a miracle and marvel to watch a child grow to comprehension and to hear his first word—"Daddy! Abba!" A man reborn in baptism (v. 12) and able to pray "Father" is a greater miracle. But here is more than regenerating, putting new life into life. Here is God making something out of nothing. "You who were dead . . . God made alive . . . having forgiven us." The canceled bond with its legal demands was nailed to the cross, and the nails went through the hands and feet of God's own Son!

Deceit at work to make a prey of you. Deity at work to make a pray-er of you. There are no limits to our conversation with God, but there are different subjects of conversation—say, "Father!" Say, "Fish." Say, "Egg." But most of all, say, "Spirit!" Say, "Holy Spirit!" (Luke 11:13).

We need not, as did the disciples, wait to ask for help until "he ceased." When we ask for the Holy Spirit, we join the praying of our Lord (John 14:15–17, 23). When we receive the Spirit, we have the answer to our request, "Teach us to pray." "He will teach you all things" (John 14:26). Say, "Spirit!" Say, "Holy Spirit!"

Abraham knew God as one who looked at Sodom and Gomorrah and said, "I will go down to see" (Gen. 18:21). Before him Abraham could only say, "Oh let not the Lord be angry" and could only go for ten (Gen. 18:32). Cannot we, will not we, for whom God has come down to die, go for five, for one—no, go for more, for the Spirit!

First Lesson: The Place of Prayer. If we would pray, we must find the place of prayer. The disciples found Jesus "praying in a certain place" (Luke 11:1). "Teach us, most of all by showing us the place of prayer—beyond righteousness and justice, in the grace of God." "For the sake of ten . . ." (Gen. 18:32)—but there were no ten. He destroyed them. He is judge of all the earth and does right. Men's wrong means God's right can only be wrath. There Sodom and Gomorrah bore that wrath. For us, Jesus did. There were none righteous, no, not one. But there was, is now, and ever shall be, One righteous, righteous in all that he did, and him God spared not, but delivered him up for us all. That is grace. And in that grace prayer can take place. "Will he not also give us all things with him?" (Rom. 8:32).

Abraham knew his place (vv. 27, 30). And when he reached the limit of even his own presumption, Abraham "returned to his place" (v. 33). Great courage? A rash risk? Damning daring, to ask for justice (v. 25), to ask the Judge of all the earth to do *right*. Use Genesis language: "Because the outcry against Selma and Grand Rapids is great and their sin is very grave, I will go down to see . . . and I will know." He came unto his own, and his own received him not, and he knew. He knew when they mocked his only Son who "came down from heaven," when they said, "If you are the Son of God, come down from the cross" (Matt. 27:40). Is it not damning to ask the Judge of all the earth, the God who knows, the God we know knows, to do *right*?

But Abraham also knew God. We look into his face and see the Judge of all the earth. We see him differently in the face of Jesus Christ—"The

Word . . . full of grace and truth" (John 1:14). We have seen *him* and so have seen the Father (John 14:9). He has given us the righteousness beyond righteousness (2 Cor. 5:21; Rom. 3:21). God did not come down to see—he came that we might see. He came to save, that we might know his love even as we are known by him in love. This knowing interchange was Abraham's as well. This is the covenant, and this is the mutual knowing between those covenantly bound together. "Abraham believed . . . he reckoned it to him as righteousness" (Gen. 15:6).

His prayer, then, was the daring of faith, faith in grace, faith in a God who made a covenant with his people. Do we know our place? Our place in grace? We do if we know God, the God of grace. "If you are Christ's, then you are Abraham's offspring, heirs according to promise" (Gal. 3:29).

Our Lord said, "If you were Abraham's children, you would do what Abraham did" (John 8:39). Do. Pray.

Second Lesson: Doing Righteousness and Justice. "Live in Christ . . . abounding in thanksgiving" (Col. 2:6–7). All that happened in the OT lesson was to help Abraham charge his children to do righteousness and justice so that God could bring to him what he had promised (Gen. 18:17–19). God has done abundantly more than we could ask or think to enable us to live in Christ.

What we can do (live in him, abounding in thanksgiving—pray!) is completely based on *what he is* (the whole fullness of deity dwells in him bodily) and on *what God has done in him* (canceled the legal demands, nailing them to his cross, and then raising him from the dead) and on *what we have become* (fully alive in him, sinful flesh cut away in Christ's circumcision, death to sin died with Christ with whom we are buried in baptism, and raised with him through faith in the working of God).

God has made us alive together with Christ Jesus. So live in him!

Gospel: The Fortunate Importunate. The importunate *needs*, and he *knows* it, and he *seeks, knocks,* and *asks* for it. He is fortunate—when?

This man knew he needed bread. He figured he needed three loaves. He sought his friend, he knocked *and* knocked (troublesomely urgent, overly persistent, that describes the importunate), he asked *and* asked, and he received. A fortunate importunate?

Something could go wrong anywhere along the line. Say he didn't know what he needed, thought he had bread and so asked for eggs. Then having sought and knocked and asked and received, he would still be an unfortunate importunate. Say he went to a breadless friend . . . say he was too bashful to knock . . . say he couldn't bring himself to ask. Unfortunate importunate.

(The sermon could work with the Lord's Prayer as a guide to what we really need. The parable could urge to persistence in prayer. The ask, seek, find trio could structure the premise, the process, and the promise of prayer. The human analogy could stress our dependable Father. But this pericope's final twist suggests another turn.)

He knew the need . . . the need was bread . . . the house was found . . . the door was knocked . . . the bread was asked . . . and then, muffled, there was the sound of a man stirring from bed, clambering over his children, bumping into the table, slamming the cupboard, unbolting the door, and suddenly thrusting into the importunate man's hands—*The Spirit! The Holy Spirit!* Fortunate importunate!

There he was—Jesus Christ, the only-begotten Son of God, sent by the Father to create a right spirit within man. Joy set before him, but hard to despise cross and shame. There they were, the twelve, representative mankind, nucleus of the new creation. "Teach us to pray—let's get our club organized at least as well as John did his."

Well, it is a good thing, to pray is. So here: "Father!" All summed up in that. But get the angles: "*Thy* name! *Thy* kingdom! *Thy* forgiveness! *Thy* perfection! yes, and *our bread.*"

And that's what they latched on to. He could see it. Bread. So all right, here is a story about bread. But look: the Father is better than any earthly father—he wants to give the good gift! Himself! The Holy Spirit! For this cause came I into the world (Col. 2:9, 13–15) . . .

"How much more will the heavenly Father give the Holy Spirit to those who ask him"—if they heard him, if we hear him now, then suddenly the door opening again, and there, thrust into our hands, *The Spirit! The Holy Spirit!* Fortunate importunates!

The Eleventh Sunday after Pentecost

Lutheran	*Roman Catholic*	*Episcopal*	*Presbyterian and UCC*
Eccles. 1:2; 2:18–26	Eccles. 1:2; 2:21–23	Eccles. 1:2; 2:18–23	Eccles. 2:18–23
Col. 3:1–11	Col. 3:1–5, 9–11	Col. 3:1–5, 9–11	Col. 3:1–11
Luke 12:13–21	Luke 12:13–21	Luke 12:13–21	Luke 12:13–21

EXEGESIS

First Lesson: Eccles. 1:2; 2:18–26. Within Ecclesiastes, 2:18–23 and 2:24–26 are the fourth and fifth discourses (of some twenty-seven); 1:2 is the motto-like introduction to the whole book, probably from a disciple of Ecclesiastes. Receiving their final form in the 3rd century B.C., the discourses debate the certainty of earlier wisdom by pointing to the experience of the fragmentary in man's life, his quest for meaning, and his attempt to grasp the whole work of God beginning to end (3:11). The Preacher makes theological affirmations and confesses that reality is beyond his grasp (7:23–24).

The discourse in 2:18–23 treats the ambiguity of leaving an inheritance. The agonizing encounter with death (2:12–17) is also manifest in the uncertainty of what becomes of one's life's work when passed on to the successor: his wisdom or foolishness may turn the legacy to blessing or curse, to good or evil. This formulation is a general observation, but the foolish squandering of Solomon's inheritance by his son Rehoboam (1 Kings 12:1–18) can serve as a case in point. Prov. 13:22 and Job 27: 16–17 show that the topic was discussed by wisdom teachers who pointed out that it was foolish to make success in acquiring goods the center and goal of one's life. Cf. Ecclus. (Jesus ben Sira) 11:18–20; Luke 12:16–20.

The gift of "the here and now" is celebrated in the next discourse (2: 24–26). The invitation to eat and drink is born neither of the thoughtless blasphemy of the cynic (cf. Isa. 22:13; 1 Cor. 15:32) nor of the despair unto death in the Babylonian "Dialogue of Pessimism" ("What, then, is good?" "To have my neck and your neck broken . . . ," lines 80–81). Ecclesiastes dares to stand where he finds himself, resting in the certainty that God is the giver of joy and life (cf. 9:7–10), even though it remains God's secret how they are apportioned.

As do the other discourses of Ecclesiastes, 2:18–23 and 2:24–26 challenge a wisdom—any wisdom—that becomes sure of itself and so hardens into "the system." The reality of the absurd both at the fringe of *and* in the center of life, is courageously perceived and not systematized away with yet another set of solutions. God's quest for man sets man free for his quest for reality (2:24); the manifestations of man's quest are to be cherished, however, as vessels which stand ready to be broken (cf. 2 Cor. 4:7).

Second Lesson: Col. 3:1–11. The passage is the first part of the hortatory section 3:1–4:6. It is preceded by a theological argument against the opponents (2:6–23) and a section in which the writer discusses Christ's lordship over the realm of the spirits (1:15–2:5). The hortatory section moves from a general exhortation to warnings against the deeds of "the old man" (3:5–11), then to admonitions to the deeds of "the new man" (3:12–17), followed by specific commands to wives, children, servants, and masters (3:18–4:1), and concludes with the general exhortation (4:2–6).

Contrary to "the opponents" of 2:6–15 who seek to earn their "full-ness" through observances (2:16), Col. 3:1–2 argues that the full Christian life is the manifestation of having risen with Christ. In Pauline theology the imperative, "Therefore live as new people," corresponds to the indicative, "you have been raised"; cf. Gal. 5:1–25. The Christian life is being "in this world, yet not of this world" (cf. John 17:16), living in the tension of "the already and the not yet" (3:3–4), neither escaping from this world nor exhausting itself in this world.

The new life manifests itself negatively in the rejection of the old man's self-centered and self-gratifying pattern of life and of the old society's self-serving pattern (3:5–11), and positively in mutual acceptance, for-bearance, and support (3:12 ff.). The two lists of things to avoid in 3:5 and 3:8, each made up of five items, are traditional (cf. Eph. 5:3, 5; 4:25 ff.) and typify the old man. For the equation of ruthless greed with idolatry see Phil. 3:19. The new man is pictured as re-created in God's image (Gen. 1:26–27), moving toward that communion with God and man for which he, the trusted creature, was called into being. That communion, now reality in the new life in Christ's body, the church, relates all baptized persons to each other as members of one body, irrespective of their station in life, sex, or race (1 Cor. 12:13; Gal. 3:26–28).

The text unfolds the Pauline unity of indicative and imperative in response and opposition to a faction within the church that reintroduces "the law in disguise." Paul's proclamation of the gospel that sets human beings free both enables and commands the manifestations of that freedom.

Gospel: Luke 12:13–21. Within the section "Jesus on the way to suffering and ascension" (9:51–18:14, a compositional element found only in Luke), 12:13–21 is one of several passages (14:7–14; 16:1–13; 16:19–31) which deal with a topic of importance to Luke: Who is *truly* rich in the period of the church that stretches from the outpouring of the Spirit to the end (Acts 2:1–4, cf. 1:8), times in which Luke's hearers find themselves? Luke 12:13–21 is introduced with a question addressed to Jesus by a man who has unsuccessfully tried to have his older brother give him his share of the paternal property (cf. 15:12; Num. 27:8–10). Jesus refuses the role of arbiter in order to state that the man who relies on the created instead of on the Creator misses life (Rom. 1:25). The request (v. 13) is rejected, not because it is illegitimate (1 Cor. 6:5!) but because it could become a disguise for securing oneself by possessions (v. 15). This point is illustrated by an example story which shows how one acts rightly.

Luke 12:16–21 treats an old theme in a new example story. Example stories (cf. Prov. 6:6–9) unfold as narratives and so illustrate one or more maxims. Luke 12:16–21 combines themes already found in Ps. 49:16–17, Ecclus. 11:18–19; 31:5, 7–8, and Prov. 11:26 into an example story. It illustrates the foolishness of hoarding what the Creator's bounty gave, and *so* wishing to secure life and future for oneself. Not the unexpected coming of death as such, but the situation its coming reveals is illustrated: a person seeking to gain life by enslaving himself to that which, created like him, is even less powerful. On "Fool!" see Ps. 14:1. Being "rich toward God" is illustrated in Luke 12:32–34 and 19:1–10.

Possessions as such are not condemned; cf. Luke 15:1–10. Avarice (1 Cor. 5:11), anxiously holding on to possessions (Acts 5:1–11), reveals what really matters to the person. Hence: "Let those . . . who buy live as though they had no goods . . ." (1 Cor. 7:29–31; cf. 1 Tim. 6:17–19 for a fully phrased warning against avarice).

HOMILETICAL INTERPRETATION

A theme for the day is *Pleasing in Thy Sight*. Once you know everything is vanity, relax and enjoy it. Many in our world hear that much from the Preacher (Eccles. 1:2) and some seem to make a good thing of life. "Nothing better," says the Preacher; but he cannot relax, because he can only equate goods and God (Eccles. 2:24). And that means if a man does not have goods, he is somehow not pleasing to God. But getting rich and gathering into barns doesn't prove a man pleasing; it may merely indicate a sinner who gathers and heaps only to yield it all in death to one who pleases God in the next generation (Eccles. 2:26). Relax? Enjoy? (Eccles. 2:26.)

Are we caught in that generation gap? And hate it? (Eccles. 2:18–19.) How can we be the man who pleases God, be rich, get knowledge, wisdom, and joy (Eccles. 2:26)? The Collect for Grace prays, "Defend us . . . that all our doings, being ordered by Thy governance, may be righteous in Thy sight." But his governance works the generation trap. How be pleasing in his sight?

You cannot force God to be pleased with you by gathering evidence of his pleasure into bulging barns (Luke 12:18). "Look at me!" "Look what I can do, Father!" Nor can you make yourself pleasing by "setting your mind" to it or "seeking" it (Col. 3:1–2).

The way to be pleasing to God is to get in with his Son, who was crucified, died, and was buried, and on the third day rose again. Die with him. Be raised with him. He is the beloved Son in whom God is well pleased. He has made us accepted in the Beloved (Eph. 1:2–7)!

First Lesson: Who Pleases God, Gets. The good life is given to the good, some claimed. Jesus played on that with his little joke: "The rich

man died—and in Hades he lifted up his eyes . . ." (Luke 16:23). "The
absurd at the fringe and in the center of life" will not let us believe that
the happy ending results from good characters. The point Jesus made was
that God must justify the heart, and that God can be found in "Moses
and the prophets" (Luke 16:14–15, 31).

Is it true that who pleases God, gets? The Preacher concludes so (2:26).
He expects the end will justify having means (vv. 24–25). But he is not
sure (v. 26). Could "the beloved Son" conclude so? "My Son in whom I
am well pleased!"—but what did he have? No place to lay his head. What
did he get? A grave with the rich, only that, only borrowed, only a three
day lease; and his one coat lost in a dice game. Still he recommends his
way to all who would be sons in the Beloved (Mark 8:34–38), and makes
his point with a reference to the opposing view such as that held by the
rich man in today's Gospel (Mark 8:36).

Still, struggling to make ends meet does not justify. The approach cannot be, "Chasten me, O God, so that you begin to love me" (Hebrews 12).
His love is primary. Whom he loves, gets—and discipline is part of it.
What is necessary is that we be justified at the end, "when he comes in
the glory" (Mark 8:38).

If we choose God for our portion (Ps. 73:26), how rich when God is
all in all!

Second Lesson: Living as One Possessed. Things we possess can
possess us. How easily we get "caught up" in things—from Scrabble or
bridge to the stock market or sex. We live like one possessed. The dic-
tionary illustrates that word with "as by a demon"; it concedes that one
could be "self-possessed"; but it offers no suggestion that one could be
"Christ possessed," "God possessed." Yet that is the urgent plea of this
word of God. "As therefore you received Christ Jesus the Lord, so live in
him" (Col. 2:6) was the beginning—we possess Christ; but this text turns
it about for the concluding argument—"you have been raised with Christ
. . . your life is hid with Christ in God." We are possessed.

Our problem areas are more extensive than covetousness (vv. 5–9, 11)
even though the theme of all the Sundays' lessons might suggest a focus
on possession by possessions. But "idolatry" sums them all up. And because they are all idolatry, we want to put them all down. It seems so
simple. If you find yourself kneeling down to wood and stone, just quit.
It is not difficult to stop worshiping. Rather easily and repeatedly we
have stopped worshiping the *true* God, why not these earthly ones? Be
serious about "possession"—the demonic must be "put to death" (v. 5).
And "the wrath of God" is coming ultimately to do just that (v. 6). Who
dares wait? But where start? How begin?

If our sermon can only talk *about* this death and *about* our life in Christ, then we are of all men most miserable. Rather wield the two-edged sword. "Wrath" as real ("Fool! This night . . . ," Luke 12:20). "Life" as the power of God to salvation!

How can the gospel be preached as a power to move us to do what God here wills us to do? Perhaps a direct series of suggestions like these will make our Lord's death and resurrection real for us. Come into the sepulcher you who have kept your possessions tightly tied in a napkin (Luke 19:20). Bind it about your head (John 11:44). Look like your Lord (John 20:7). "You have died, and your life is hid with Christ in God" (v. 3). Quick! You are! For he is! (Rom. 8:11; Eph. 2:1, 4–7). Here, in the darkness of this present world, before the stone is hurled away and "Christ who is our life appears!" Live like the living Lord. It is but a short time—till the third day. Put the old nature aside there on the slab. Put on the new nature, renewed! "We are God's children now!" (1 John 3:2–3). Be ready—when the stone is rolled back (John 16:5) shall we be found there, sitting on the right side, dressed in a white robe, renewed after the image of our creator?

Gospel: Parceling Our Possessions. Where do you budget God? Does he, and do the least of the brothers of his Son, find a place at the bottom of your budget figures among the miscellaneous? The Lord's story makes clear we'd better not try to store our possessions in a big new barn. No lightning rod for the soul! The Lord seems to avoid answering the parceling out problem (v. 14). A typical sermon cop-out? But this man was "one of the multitude" and his brother was not with him. We are not to judge "the greedy and robbers, or idolaters . . . but anyone who bears the name of brother, if he is guilty of immorality or greed—not even to eat with such a one" (1 Cor. 5:9–13). We who together eat and drink the body and blood of our Lord ought to help one another wrap our parcels.

The Lord came into life with an economic hymn (Luke 1:53) and judged—better, instructed—his followers about possessions (Luke 5:11; 6:20, 30–31; 9:3; 12:32 ff.; etc.). Shall we say about the brother, "It's his bag" (John 12:6), "It's his business" (John 13:29)? "The best construction" on his parceling performance may contribute to his destruction.

There's only so much to go around, correct. Rich toward God (v. 21) must mean less treasure for self. But there is no use threatening, "He is a hard God" (Matt. 25:24), and no use exhorting by example, even by our Lord's (Luke 9:58). Greed is dispelled by preached gospel, covetousness by the Word, Christ. The word is not "Be good" but God's goodness that makes good—the grace of our Lord Jesus Christ (2 Cor. 8:8–10).

The Twelfth Sunday after Pentecost

Lutheran	*Roman Catholic*	*Episcopal*	*Presbyterian and UCC*
Gen. 15:1–6	Sap. 18:6–9	Gen. 15:1–6	2 Kings 17:33–40
Heb. 11:1–3, 8–16	Heb. 11:1–2, 8–19	Heb. 11:1–2, 8–16	Heb. 11:1–3, 8–12
Luke 12:32–40	Luke 12:32–48	Luke 12:32–40	Luke 12:35–40

EXEGESIS

First Lesson: Gen. 15:1–6. This passage is part of the story of "the Fathers," Abraham, Isaac, Jacob, and his twelve sons (Genesis 12–50), which, in turn, is the prologue to Israel's recital of its deliverance from slavery to freedom (Exodus 1–Deuteronomy 34). In Genesis 15 the older (Jerusalem-Judah based) tradition of a covenant between the Lord and Abram which sealed the patron-god relationship between the two (15:7–21 J), is prefaced by a more prophetically oriented, Northern introduction which seeks to supply theological keys for the Abram covenant.

Already in the earliest historical traditions the Lord's work began with promises given to "wandering Arameans," land-hungry nomads at the fringes of the desert. For the Jerusalem-Judah centered Southerners the first recipient of the divine call was Abram (Gen. 12:1–3 J); his call was confirmed by covenant (15:7–21 J). In 15:1–6, however, a prophetically oriented perspective surfaces: the Lord's *word* comes in *a vision* to Abram at night, and he responds *in faith* even though the evidence speaks against it (Abram had not one child so far!). If, as most students think, the Northern-prophetic strand of the Pentateuch (E = the Elohistic work) began with Gen. 15:1–6, then its recital of Israel's origins did not begin with a creation story (as in the Pentateuchal strand from the hands of wise men [J] or of priestly circles [P]), but it began with a promise delivered as prophetic word and as command to history: let there be numerous descendants of Abram—let there be the people of the Lord. Here Abram is distinguished as the father of a holy people, father by power of the word of the Lord. Abram's evident childlessness, of which every hearer is painfully aware, contrasts starkly with Abram's response: "faith" is that attitude and action which is anchored in the Lord's promised, and therefore sure, action in present and future; cf. Isa. 7:9. The Lord, in turn, responds by "reckoning it" to Abram "as righteousness," a theologically weighted term which is based on an originally cultic technical phrase: with it a priest confirms the validity of a sacrifice; cf. Lev. 17:4. "Righteousness" does not refer to an abstract, absolute norm; it is

that action and attitude which manifests the mutuality and loyalty of covenantal relationships; cf. Ezek. 18:5–9.
The Elohistic emphasis evident in Gen. 15:1–6, on Abram as "our father," on his response in "faith" which is his "righteousness," and on the people of the Lord as that which the Lord promises and so creates through his word, balances the more land and possession based Yahwistic view of Abram, first recipient of the promise of the land.

Second Lesson: Heb. 11:1–3, 8–16. The theological treatise entitled "To the Hebrews" has its center in the section 7:1–10:18. Going beyond elementary instruction, it unfolds the thesis: Christ, high priest after the order of Melchizedek, is, in contrast to the temporary and shadow-like priesthood of the Old Covenant, mediator of the New, the final and real covenant (Platonic contrast!). Jesus has once for all offered the all-sufficient sacrifice and has entered the heavenly temple forever. The unique feature of this thesis in early Christianity is the interpretation of cross and exaltation in *cultic* terms. Heb. 10:19–12:29 is an exhortation based on this thesis. Chap. 11 intervenes. It is a list of OT illustrations on the theme of "faith," based on the Septuagint version of Hab. 2:3–4 (Heb. 10:38, as interpreted in 10:39).

Thesis-like, the compact formulation in 11:1–2 begins an excursus on "faith" by boldly *identifying* it with that which is anticipated: God's reality is present in the suffering Jesus (Heb. 1:3; 5:7) *and* in the faith of the congregation (11:1). Hence, faith is not (subjectively) an assurance concerning something beyond the faithful but is the presence of the invisible. In Israel's ancestors that faith was manifest although for them it was not yet fully present reality (11:2; cf. 11:13).

The discussion of the reality of faith (11:1–2) is followed by a listing of manifestations of faith (11:3, 8–12). Each entry on the list (similar lists are known from Jewish-Hellenistic synagogue proceedings: 4 Macc. 1: 1–7; 3:19 ff., cf. Acts 7:2 ff.) opens with the words "by/in faith." Heb. 11:3 is unusual in that the writer includes himself with his hearers as those who perceive the world (universe, lit.: aeons) to have come into being through the word of the Lord (Gen. 1:1–2:4a: order out of chaos at God's command, contrast Heb. 11:3b: being out of nonbeing at God's command). Several Abraham traditions are summarized as manifestations of his faith (but Gen. 15:6 where the word actually occurs, is not mentioned): his obedience to the call (Gen. 12:1–4a), his sojourning in Canaan as resident alien (Gen. 23:4), and his acceptance of the promise of Isaac's birth against human expectations (Gen. 18:11–14; 21:3).

In the priestly strand of the Pentateuch Abraham is pictured as merely a sojourner in Canaan, not yet as possessor of the land of promise (Gen.

23:3 P, cf. Exod. 6:2–9 P). Hebrews reinterprets this motif so that the
sojourn of Abraham shows him to be on the move toward a greater
country, "I mean, the heavenly one" (cf. 11:10).

The intent of the writer is to stress the finality and fullness of God's
presence in Christ's suffering *and* in the congregation's faith by showing
it to be the climax of preliminary manifestations of that faith among the
ancestors of Israel.

Gospel: Luke 12:32–40. These verses are sectioned in this manner in
the RSV and NEB, but differently in JB. They are part of a Lucan didac-
tic composition which draws on Q and L (the Lucan source). The wider
context is 9:51–18:14, the unique Lucan arrangement of Q, L, and some
Marcan traditions, which shows Jesus on his way from Galilee to Jerusalem, journeying, as it were, toward cross and exaltation. Jesus on his
pilgrimage teaches in 12:32–40 how Christians as a minority are to live
confidently, wisely, and expectantly during the period of the church
which stretches from Jesus' exaltation toward the end.

Only Luke among the Synoptics has the exhortation, directed to "the
little flock, not to be afraid" (v. 32) which highlights the minority status
of the Christian congregation after Jesus' exaltation. In the matter of dis-
cretionary possessions the church's stance is clear: not earthly security
but being "rich with God" is the guiding principle (vv. 33–34; cf. Matt.
6:19–21). Contrast with this the foolish behavior of the rich farmer (Luke
12:16–21, see Pentecost 11) and of Ananias and Sapphira (Acts 4:36–
5:11). Man's heart is the seat of his will, emotions, and rational powers
(cf. 2 Sam. 7:3; Prov. 26:25). In contrast to Matt. 6:21 Luke employs the
plural ("your [pl.] heart"): the disciples are not seen individually but
collectively, that is, the community of the church is envisaged.

Christian existence is described as continually being on one's toes (12:
35–40). This description unfolds in a twofold way: the parable (and
macarism, cf. Matt. 5:3–10) of the servants who are ready for their master's return no matter when he arrives (35–38, cf. Mark 13:33–37; Matt.
25:1–13) and the parable of the unknown nightly moment when the
burglar strikes (39–40; cf. Matt. 24:43–44). Both parables interpret for
the early Christians the coming of "the Son of man" (title of an apocalyptic heavenly figure who is expected to appear as universal judge and
to usher in God's universal and manifest rule, cf. Dan. 7:13–14; Acts
7:55–56).

Girded loins signify readiness to act (Exod. 12:11), lit lamps prepared-
ness (cf. Matt. 25:7–8). The returned master reverses the roles and serves
his slaves (37*b*)—this is an allegorical feature referring to Christ's servant-
hood (Mark 10:45; John 13:1–20). In the first parable (and indirectly in

the second) waking manifests loyalty and solidarity, falling asleep the opposite (cf. the Gethsemane story, Mark 14:32–42 par.). Luke directs the exhortation specifically to the leaders of the congregation; cf. Peter's question (12:41) and the parable of the trusted steward which stands as answer (12:42–46).

HOMILETICAL INTERPRETATION

A theme for the day is *Believing Is Pleasing*. What a joy—so to live that God will say, "He's a good man!" (Gen. 15:6). So to live that God will not be ashamed to be called our God (Heb. 11:16)! So to live that God himself will gird an apron about him and have us sit at table and come and serve us (Luke 12:37)!

What a fear—that we fail and fall into the hands of the living God (Heb. 10:29–31). Abram knew that fear (Gen. 15:1), and the disciples knew it (Luke 12:32). Sarah tried to laugh it off (Gen. 18:12) and the last thing the Lord said as he left the tent of Abram was, "No, but you did laugh" (Gen. 18:15). You did, you know . . . and of us it must be said as of the Israelites, "with most of them God was not pleased" (1 Cor. 10:5). Baptized, communing, gathering-in-the-tabernacle Christians, "these things are warnings for us." "The Son of man is coming in an hour you do not expect" (Luke 12:40).

What a gift—that God gives us the very thing with which, when we receive it, he is well pleased. "I am your shield" and for everything *I* do for you, *you* will be greatly rewarded (Gen. 15:1)! Abram believed the Lord. That's all. "And he reckoned it to him as righteousness" (Gen. 15:6). What a deal! Faith—"by it the men of old received divine approval" (Heb. 11:2). "It is your Father's good pleasure to give you the kingdom" (Luke 12:32). Unbelievable!

It really is. And to make himself credible to the incredulous, God gave the world to us all (Heb. 11:3), gave Isaac to Abram (Gen. 21:2), but best of all, gave the promised Jesus Christ to all men.

Believing the promise pleases God. And in the promise is the power to believe. "I am not ashamed of the Gospel"—by it God is not ashamed to be called my God (Rom. 1:16–17).

First Lesson: Faith Is What Counts. Think of the years Abraham spent counting, waiting for the promise's fulfillment. "Seventy-five and still counting" about the time of this text. "Ninety-nine and still counting" when Sarah became pregnant. And then the command to sacrifice his son, his only son, Isaac, and his counting voice almost lost cadence. And finally, still counting, he died, in faith, but "not having received

The King's Library

what was promised" (Heb. 11:13). But during all those years of counting
"he believed the Lord; and the Lord reckoned it to him as righteousness"
(v. 6).

Faith is what counts—therefore God is not ashamed to be called the
God of Abraham, Isaac, and Jacob. And therefore God would be pleased
to be known as the God of you and me.

Faith counts on God. Justification by faith—Romans 4.

Faith stands up and is counted. Faith without works is dead—James
2:18–26.

The full count includes us who believe—Rom. 9:6–32; Gal. 3:1–9!

Second Lesson: Faith Presses to Bring off the Promise. God made
a great promise. Can he bring it off? Not without us! From us, with all
these men of faith, God hopes for endurance that he might bring it off
(Heb. 10:36–39). The great cloud of witnesses, "well attested by their
faith, did not receive what was promised, since God had forseen something better for us" (Heb. 12:1; 11:39–40). He is saving the completion
of the promise—for us!

Faith at a minimum (Heb. 11:6; Gen. 15:1) and faith extended (Heb.
11:1) looks "to Jesus, the pioneer and perfecter of our faith" (Heb. 12:2),
to his redeeming cross, his exaltation at the right hand of God; faith
awaits his triumphant return (Luke 12:40), at which the world will be
shaken (Heb. 12:26), and in the unshakable kingdom God will bring into
fulfillment all that he has promised (Heb. 10:36; 11:39–40).

The Jewish Christians, tottering toward backsliding, and we all, are
warned against shrinking back before the coming one comes (Heb. 10:
37–38)! We are urged to be men and women of faith who endure and
press forward in faith to receive all that is promised by God. God would
be ashamed of us if we would fail to appreciate the better country, the
heavenly one, which he has prepared for us.

Pound in the tent pegs each evening with Abraham, Isaac, and Jacob;
but remember you are one day's journey nearer home, nearer the city
which has foundations, whose builder and maker is God (v. 10).

Not yet, but already "you have come to the city of the living God
because you have come to Jesus, the mediator of a new covenant" (Heb.
12:22–24).

Gospel: To Please God More and More. St. Paul besought and exhorted the Thessalonians in the Lord Jesus, "As you learned from us how
you ought to live and to please God, just as you are doing, you do so
more and more" (1 Thess. 4:1).

His appeal is "in the Lord Jesus." He is the Son who makes God the
Father well pleased and makes it his pleasure to give the little flock the

kingdom (Luke 12:32). What the Father wants, our goal should be that the Father gets. He gets it as we accept by faith. The man who does not live by faith, who shrinks back, "my soul has no pleasure in him" (Heb. 10:38). It is the Father's pleasure to give—when we are really and continually ready to receive, He goes all out and waits on us. What a great way to be living—constantly being given to! Faith is putting your heart where your Lord is—making the Lord your treasure.

We please God as we do his will, which is our sanctification (1 Thess. 4:3–12). "Sell your possessions and give alms" (v. 33) but remember it is nothing if we do not love (1 Cor. 13:3). We please God more and more as more and more we love, gird loins, light our lamps, stay awake, and "open to him at once when he comes and knocks" (vv. 36, 40).

The Thirteenth Sunday after Pentecost

Lutheran	Roman Catholic	Episcopal	Presbyterian and UCC
Jer. 23:23–29	Jer. 38:4–6, 8–10	Jer. 23:23–29	Jer. 38:1b–13
Heb. 12:1–13	Heb. 12:1–4	Heb. 12:1–4	Heb. 12:1–6
Luke 12:49–53	Luke 12:49–53	Luke 12:49–56	Luke 12:49–53

EXEGESIS

First Lesson: Jer. 23:23–29. Toward the end of the first part of the Book of Jeremiah (1–25) appear two appendix-like collections of words and comments which deal with the royal house (21:11–23:8) and with Jeremiah's fellow prophets (23:9–40). The last collection contributes to the emerging Jeremiah tradition (Jeremiah 36!), sayings uttered by the prophet about fellow prophets from whom he knows himself to be set apart or with whom he finds himself in strong disagreement (cf. 5:10–13; 2:8; 28:1–17). The section 23:23–29 can be set off more easily from what precedes than from what follows: RSV prints 23–32 as one prose unit; JB offers 23–24 as poetry, 25–28a as prose, 28b–29 as poetry, 30–32 as prose; NEB has 23–24 as poetry (as part of the unit 16–24) and 25–32 as prose.

Vv. 23–32 may be taken as the opening of a lawsuit which brings disloyal prophets before their sovereign for judgment: vv. 23–24—the confrontation; vv. 25–29—the examination and declaration of guilt; vv. 30–32—the announcement of imminent punishment. The opening words (vv. 23–24) affirm that the Lord cannot be confined by a prophet to a controllable and comfortable nearness (Ps. 139:2–12), a closeness which is misrepresented by certain prophets as his imminent deliverance from the threats to the nation's existence as experienced now in the last decades of the kingdom of Judah (cf. Jeremiah's words against prophets who speak "peace, peace" when there is no peace [6:14; 8:11]; also 28:1–17). The conflicts with other prophets raise for Jeremiah the question of the criterion of the true prophet. In 28:8–9 we find him searching for such a criterion in tradition, that is, he there argues that only *that* prophet of peace is a true prophet whose word does become reality—in distinction from the (earlier) prophets of doom whose word did not require such proof. In vv. 25–29 Jeremiah finds the criterion in the mode of revelation (if dreams are the medium, then it is merely man's word) and in the result of the word (if it makes the people "forget the Lord" as the apostasy to the Canaanite fertility god Baal did, it cannot be the Lord's word). The relation of the (genuine) divine word imparted to the prophet when he stands in the heavenly council (cf. 23:18) to the dream as source of a prophet's message is compared to that of wheat to chaff: the one basic to life and health, the other useless and a nuisance. For the further comparison of the Lord's word to fire and hammer see 5:14; 1:9–10. For the "Word of the Lord" theology which also this Jeremiah-word attests cf. further Isa. 40:6–8 and 55:10–11.

Jeremiah's search for a tangible criterion of the truth of the Lord's word did not reach one final answer (cf. also Deut. 18:21–22); the bearers of that word will be and can be not more than signs and portents (Isa. 8:18) who share the hiddenness of God's presence among men.

Second Lesson: Heb. 12:1–13. (For the general context of this passage, see the introductory comments on the Second Lesson for Pentecost 12.) Heb. 12:1–13 takes up the theme of 10:32–36: "Remember the days gone by, when, nearly enlightened, you met the challenge of great suffering," and discusses further the topic of suffering.

Christ, the enabler (12:1–3), is the first line of hortatory argument: Jesus, who through his perfect and complete high priestly work has once for all made faith perfect (2:10; 5:9; 6:20), enables his followers to journey on the long road toward the final attainment of peace and righteousness (12:11). This journey is described as a race. It is a mirror-like reflection and consequence of the race run by Jesus: instead of the joy of remaining forever in the Father's presence (Phil. 2:5–9; 2 Cor. 8:9), Jesus chose to run the agonizing course of his mission unto death and life. That race brought him to the exaltation at God's right hand (Ps. 110:1) as pioneer and perfecter of our faith (12:2). Running that race is the comprehensive description of the Christian's life; all that seeks to cling to him and hold him back is "sin."

Divine pedagogy (12:4–12[13]) unfolds the hortatory argument by way of an exegesis of an OT text; the interpretation of Prov. 3:11–12 is an instructive sample of early Christian hermeneutic. Hebrews answers the question: "How can God let us, his children, suffer?" in concert with OT (Deut. 8:5; Job 5:17–27) and intertestamental (2 Macc. 6:16; Ps. Sol. 3:3–10) thought, with the comforting assertion: suffering is sent by God as chastisement and hence is further proof that those chastised are indeed God's children. Note that the affirmation that Christians are daughters and sons of God is here based on their creatureliness; cf. Isa. 64:8; Mal. 2:10; but contrast Rom. 8:14–17.

Hebrews stresses that as faith exhibits its most genuine quality in "perseverance," in "continuing" (John 8:34–35), so sin becomes manifest as "slackening." Reminiscent of Luke's description of the life of the Christian during the period of the church or of the Holy Spirit, Hebrews interprets Christian life as "the journey home," agonizing now but clear and certain in its goal.

Gospel: Luke 12:49-53. Luke 12:49–50, 51–53 is part of the unique Lucan composition 9:51–18:14 which draws mostly on Q and L (the Lucan source). It shows Jesus "on the way to Cross and Exaltation," demonstrating in both his teaching and his actions oriented "toward Jerusalem" (9:51) how Christians are to shape their life in the period of the church, ushered in and sustained by the gift of the Spirit (Acts 1:8; 2:1–13).

The fire of the Spirit (12:49–50) is a Lucan extension and interpretation of an older tradition which sets forth Jesus' martyr-death as "baptism" (so Mark 10:38). Looking forward to that agonizing "baptism" "greatly distressed" Jesus (12:50b, JB); the Gethsemane story highlights this especially for Luke who is interested in Jesus also as the exemplary martyr. The word of the Lucan Jesus affirming that he came to throw fire on the earth, unparalleled in the other Gospels, is probably to be interpreted against the backdrop of Luke's theology: the fire Jesus is to cast is the coming and the ensuing presence of the Spirit "like tongues of fire" (Acts 2:3) in the midst of the Christian congregation. Less likely interpretations: the fire as purifier of human beings for the coming kingdom of God (Luke 3:16–17) or as the agent of judgment (Rev. 20:10).

The word of Jesus referring to himself (12:51–53) quotes and interprets Mic. 7:6 as response to what obviously was a pressing issue in the early churches (cf. Matt. 10:34–36): If Jesus is the eschatological bringer of "peace" (Luke 2:14; 19:42; Acts 10:36; cf. John 14:27; Eph.

2:14), why does his coming and the gospel in which he continues to come, split families? In answer to *that* question the Jesus of Q (the collection of sayings and teachings centered in the coming kingdom of God and current in early Palestinian Christian congregations) interprets and expands a text found in the prophetic books. There, in Mic. 7:1–6, a lament over universal injustice in the land, mistrust even within the circle of the family is described as yet another sign of the breakdown of covenantal loyalty. Jesus, according to Luke, had already in an exemplary fashion set forth the criterion as to who is his mother and brother (8:19–21; cf. Mark 3:21). Small wonder that his followers had to face the same issue and find that the very gospel of peace sets them against members of their families.

Luke safeguards the gospel's promise and bringing of "peace" against a misunderstanding: it is not to be mistaken for letting a broken and self-centered world and mankind remain undisturbed and be at ease with themselves. The gospel does not speak of "cheap peace" (cf. John 16:33).

HOMILETICAL INTERPRETATION

A theme for the day is *God Divides to Conquer.* Diversity is a divine idea. But division—that is the metastasizing of selfishness, separatism, sin. God says, "Gesundheit"—health and wholeness. Man says, "Apartheid." But the Father does not cry, "Peace! peace!" He knows there is no peace. Instead he sends his Son, the Great Divider, the piece maker, to cut clean and so heal and make whole.

A Xerox machine creates no art. At best—an "identical crisis." Artists pull only a limited edition from an engraving or a lithograph and destroy the original. Man is a creation of the greatest Artist. God did not fold up primal matter, sheets of *Urstoff,* and then cut a pattern which he unfolded into a chain of identical paper dolls. Diversity is part of man. Each human being is himself in his distinctness and each man is to love his brother across the diversity.

But man cut himself off from God and, separated from the life source, gangrenously, rotted away from brothers and sisters. In Adam's fall we sinned all. Noah couldn't put us together again. The covenant was God's move that all nations of the earth might be blessed. But Israel divided— Jeremiah made clear that it was the word of the Lord like a hammer that broke his own people in pieces, that was a fire to burn up the straw and fill God's granary with uncommon wheat (Jer. 23:28–29).

Jesus wept about it—"I came to gather together, and you would not" (Luke 13:34). But in the Gospel he makes his method clear. He divides to conquer. He was the one whole Man come to cut clearly the division which necessarily must precede healing and ultimate wholeness (Luke 12:52; Heb. 4:12).

John the Baptizer had it right (Luke 3:16–17). Jesus came with the baptism of Spirit and fire to divide chaff and wheat. He made it clear that all men were to love one another across the chasms of their diversity. He loved all men that way. And since his words and his living were constant accusations against the selfishness and separating-ness of men, he was "cut off out of the land of the living, stricken for the transgression of his people" (Isa. 53:8). The "pioneer and perfecter of our faith, for the joy that was set before him endured the cross" (Heb. 12:2). He could not wait for his own baptism of fire to be accomplished (Luke 12:50) so that the Spirit's tongues of fire could be distributed to men (Acts 2:3; John 16:7). That loving unto death is God's conquering power.

Blessed are the piece makers—we too are to run the race our Lord set before us. Though we be called upon to endure hostility from sinners (Heb. 12:3), we are not to grow faint-hearted. "It is for discipline that you have to endure. . . . He disciplines us for our good that we may share his holiness" (Heb. 12:7, 10).

First Lesson: Remember the Name. An age that gives God as many opportunities to forgive as possible since he seems to be so eager to do so needs to hear this message. No man can hide himself from God's knowledge. A prophet who diminishes the condemning, judging word of God, is no true prophet, no true shepherd (Jer. 6:14; 8:11; 23:1–2). "I myself will fight against you with outstretched hand and strong arm, in anger, and in fury, and in great wrath" (Jer. 21:5; chaps. 22, 23 passim). "Behold, I will attend to you for your evil doings, says the Lord" (23:2). Anything short of this realistic understanding of God's stance "makes my people forget my name" (23:27).

The Lord himself will replace the false shepherds and gather the remnant of his flock (23:3). He will raise up for David a righteous Branch . . . "and this is the name by which he will be called: 'The Lord is our righteousness' " (23:5–6). Jesus came with fire and division (Luke 12:49–51) to make perfectly clear where people stood in relation to the holy God. But then he took our place under the wrath of God, the perfect one made sin for us, that we might become the righteousness of God in him (2 Cor. 5:21).

Second Lesson: The Race in Grace. The hostility which Jesus Christ aroused is well nigh unbelievable. The KJV translates, "such contradiction of sinners"—and that reveals the cause. Jesus asserted that we should love all men, even our enemies, and be merciful even as the Father is merciful (Luke 6:27–36). He made clear to those asking, "What shall I do to inherit eternal life?" that they were completely unable to "justify themselves" (Luke 10:25–37). He said to them, "You are those who justify yourselves before men, but God knows your hearts" (Luke 16: 15). The man who humbles himself before God and accepts God's mercy to the sinner will go to his house justified (Luke 18:14). He made clear that only by his dying for the sinners of the world would they know forgiveness and eternal life (9:22, 44; 12:50). This is what divided the saints from the sinners. And sinners contradicted him, on every point.

We are not above the Master. We will know the same contradiction of sinners. We ought to be sure that the contradiction is not by the saints. We must be sure that the contradiction be against a stance of love, and not a complaint because we do not practice what we preach. We lay aside every weight, every sin, that would keep us from the pace our Lord has set.

The Christian race is cross-country—long distance. It is not a dash. It is not marked by an "every day in every way I am getting holier and holier" as much as an every day we run by faith in God's grace, we run with perseverance, we run to obtain (1 Cor. 9:24) what Christ has already won for us.

Gospel: Division of the House. The angels who sang "on earth peace" (Luke 2:14) might with equal truth have sung, "on earth division." The Spirit gave Simeon understanding: "Lord, now you are permitting *me* to take my departure in peace"; but to Mary, "A sword will pierce through your own soul also"; and about the Child, "This child is set for the fall and rising of many in Israel" (Luke 2:34–35). Jesus is the point of decision, of division. It was long division viewed over the centuries of Israel's history (Jeremiah 21–23); but it is short division now—"henceforth, in one house; father-son; mother-daughter; in-law against in-law." Within those relationships and within that span of generations, decision will divide, the "falling and the rising."

"The little Lord Jesus lay down his sweet head . . . " Perhaps then. But uneasy lies the head that wears the Spirit. Here the Head of the church announces that he had come to cast fire upon the earth. Gabriel foretold the fulfilling Spirit (Luke 1:15). The Spirit descended upon Jesus at his baptism (3:22); and thereafter Jesus was led by the Spirit (4:1) into wilderness and temptation and self-offering. John the Baptizer announced that the Christ would baptize with the Holy Spirit and with fire (3:16). First he would undergo his own dreadful suffering and death (Mark 10:38–39), a baptism he was both uptight about and eager for. Then he would cast fire on the earth (Acts 2:1–4), a fire to separate the false from the true (Luke 3:17; Matt. 10:34–39).

Uneasy our heads too, upon whom the Spirit has come. We cannot take our ease in Zion, relaxed in the house of the Lord. Jesus here calls for division of the house. It is among the house of Israel that division will be made. It is among those who claimed to be servants of God in the house of the Lord that the cutting word will be spoken (Luke 20: 17–19). We who perceive ourselves as members of the household of God must be alert to the call for division (1 Cor. 10:12). The issue is Jesus Christ, and the decisions confront us not only in honoring him as we honor the Father, but in doing for the least of his brothers what we are ready to do for him (John 5:22–23; Matt. 25:40).

On the other hand, we can rest easy. The call for division which Jesus makes is aimed at passing the motion, winning his objective, saving those who believe (John 3:17–21). The score may be close—three to two and two to three—but the winners whose decision is for Jesus Christ will know his peace (John 16:33).

The Fourteenth Sunday after Pentecost

Lutheran	*Roman Catholic*	*Episcopal*	*Presbyterian and UCC*
Isa. 66:18–23	Isa. 66:18–23	Isa. 66:18b–23	Isa. 66:18–23
Heb. 12:18–24	Heb. 12:5–7, 11–13	Heb. 12:5–7, 11–13	Heb. 12:7–13
Luke 13:22–30	Luke 13:22–30	Luke 13:22–30	Luke 13:22–30

EXEGESIS

First Lesson: Isa. 66:18–23. Isaiah 56–66 is a cluster of early postexilic "prophetic" words which are centered in Isaiah 60–62 (Third Isaiah). They reflect beliefs, hopes, and fears of those Jews who, whether still in dispersion or returned to Jerusalem and Judah, uphold the memory of Isaiah of Babylon (Second Isaiah; Isaiah 40–55) and share with that prophet a theological perspective largely shaped by Isaiah of Jerusalem (8th cent. B.C.; Isaiah 1–39). Many passages of Isaiah 56–66 are reinterpretations of words, motifs, and topics found in the traditions stemming from First or Second Isaiah—in keeping with the preserving and exegeting interests of postexilic "prophetic" (apocalyptic) circles.

In contrast to Jerusalem, temple, and cult-centered priestly circles (exemplified by the Chroniclers' "creed," 2 Chron. 13:5–12) with their emphasis on Jewish particularism, legitimate priesthood, and cultic orthopraxy, certain other groups among whom the prophetic heritage was cherished and actualized, tended to stress the universal scope of the Lord's claim on Israel and mankind, the share of "all flesh" in the blessing mediated through Israel (Gen. 12:3!), and the openness of temple and worship to all. This emphasis is (polemically?) unfolded in 66:18–24: Isa. 45:20–25 and 49:6 speak of the people's coming to worship the one, true God and of the suffering servant's mission to be "the light of the nations"; in 66:18–24 a postexilic "Isaianic" interpreter takes up these motifs, affirms them, and goes beyond them by making these nations, like an unmistakable sign, messengers of the Lord's glory to those farthest away. These nations will converge on Mount Zion (cf. Isa. 25: 6–12), bringing dispersed Jews home to their holy city like an offering (cf. Isa. 49:22–23). Thus Jews and Gentiles coming to worship in Jerusalem become one new people of the Lord; from them God will select priests and Levites—an affront to the genealogy and legitimacy conscious Zadokites!

No one is excluded by reason of birth from the full celebration of sacramental signs that mark the Jew: Sabbath and New Moon (Gen. 2:1–3; Isa. 1:12–13; Num. 28:11–15; also Zech. 14:16). They all, a people newly constituted through a new exodus and a final pilgrimage to Mount Zion, are addressed by the promise that their name and descendants will forever stand, just like the new earth and the new heaven of which these emerging apocalyptic circles love to speak (Isa. 65:17; contrast Gen. 1:1–2:4a P and 9:12–17).

We can summarize by saying that nascent apocalyptic circles protest an emerging particularistic, temple, cult, and legitimacy oriented Judaism, yet are themselves prone to dualistic theologizing. Their stress on the universal scope of God's will upholds a central motif of the OT.

Second Lesson: Heb. 12:18–24. (For the general context of this passage, see the introductory comments on the Second Lesson for Pentecost 12.) After an excursus (11:1–40) on "faith" and a first hortatory argument on "the pedagogy of perseverance" (see the comments on the Second Lesson for Pentecost 13), 12:14–29 offers a second exhortation: do not reject the New Covenant!

Within the second exhortation, vv. 18–24 are a theological aside, introduced by "For . . . " and based on the contrast of the (now superseded) covenant mediated through Moses at Mount Sinai with the (final and perfect) New Covenant mediated through Jesus at Mount Zion.

The contrast (developed from a Pauline perspective in Gal. 4:24–26) is based on an allegorical interpretation of the Sinai covenant motifs; certain circumstances of its initiation correspond to certain of its characteristic features *and* contrast with their equivalents in the New Covenant. Thus (1) the Old Covenant was initiated merely at a tangible, earthly mountain—the New Covenant is consummated at a heavenly one (= Mount Zion); (2) the initiation of the Old Covenant was accompanied by dread and fear while the New Covenant is an invitation to a joyful, festal assembly; (3) the Old Covenant evoked from those addressed the frightened request not to have to listen to more divine words (contrast the positive interpretation of this feature in Deut. 5:22–28) while the New Covenant constitutes the new people of God through the gospel eagerly received in faith (Heb. 4:2).

The listings of words and phrases (a) describing the fearful features of the Old Covenant and (b) highlighting the character of the heavenly worshipers (cf. Rev. 4:1–6) are designed to have a cumulative effect; hence the meaning of some cannot be ascertained with certainty (for instance, are the "witnesses" of 11:1–40 mentioned? If so, are they the "first-born sons" and heavenly citizens or the saints who have been made perfect?).

This theological support of the exhortation in 12:14–29 sets forth a *cultic* interpretation of the newly constituted people of God, brought into being through Jesus' high priestly work.

Gospel: Luke 13:22–30. (For the general context of this passage, see the introductory remarks on the Gospel for Pentecost 13.)

This unit is a Lucan clustering and interpretation of Jesus' sayings which, as the parallels found in Matthew (7:13–14; 7:22–23; 8:11–12) show, he received from Q (a collection of sayings and teachings centered in the coming kingdom of God and alive in Palestinian Christian circles). Luke's emphasis is evident in v. 22 which sets these words of the Master into the context of his "journey toward Jerusalem." The evangelist illustrates by this arrangement and interpretation of Jesus' words that the kingdom, already present (Luke 17:20–21), is neither a "rip-off" (vv. 23–24) nor a privilege to which one may lay claim on the basis of mere acquaintance with or just friendly feeling toward Jesus (vv. 25–27) nor on the basis of being by birth a fellow Jew (vv. 28–30). In Jewish apocalyptic thought the age to come was to bring far-reaching reversals; this is reflected in Luke's theology of "entry into the kingdom." Speculations as to the number of people to enter the new age are attested; e.g., 2 Esdras (4 Ezra) 8:1, 3. Here they surface in the question directed to Jesus "by someone" (v. 23). Jesus' answer (v. 24) moves away from that speculative plane to that of the human will and of single-minded obedience to God's will (see Matt. 13:3–23; 25:31–46 for parable illustrations).

That one cannot lay claim to the kingdom on the basis of being a fellow Jew of Jesus, "a child of Abraham" (Matt. 3:9!), is starkly illustrated by an expanded parable fragment (cf. Matt. 25:10): the time will come when it is too late for entry. Then there will only be opportunity to have the exclusion of the late comers, against their strong protests (vv. 25b–26), confirmed (v. 27). They will merely be permitted to view through a hole in the door that eschatological banquet where Jews and Gentiles, "a new Israel," feast (Isa. 25:6–12; 2:2–4; Gen. 12:3; cf. also Matt. 8:11–12). Thus the Jews who were "first," turn out to be last (but, by implication, will finally also partake in the feast). For the time being, their angry response is "wailing and grinding of teeth" (here not a gesture of repentance, it seems).

Thus, in Luke's realized presence of the kingdom it cannot be "business as usual"; those who speculate on membership statistics or bank on inherited claims are bound to find themselves turned upside down.

HOMILETICAL INTERPRETATION

A theme for the day is *You Have It Made.* Gentle Jesus and the pale Galilean have disappeared, replaced by Jesus the real man. But in the process *God* has somehow been unmanned in popular thought. He is now gentle God, less in reference to gentle men than apparently to gentle Ben, the tame bear of TV. Bears danced in the Middle Ages, but under chains. It has taken our age to claim that "bear" is basically "teddy" and God no God of wrath.

In the Gospel for today God is pictured as a householder who shuts doors. When the innkeeper did as much against Joseph and Mary seeking space for the birth of God's Son, he earned a not-to-be-envied place in history. But God says more. He says, "I do not know where you come from, you workers of iniquity. Depart! There is a place where you can weep and gnash your teeth." This is not a neutral God hanging a "No vacancy" sign outside the celestial motel, no *concièrge* saying, "*complet.*" There is room—you can see through the hole in the door. And strangers from all directions have been let in. No—God, gentle God, excludes. Isaiah knew it and said so (Isa. 66:17 and 24). Moses saw God and said, "I tremble with fear" (Heb. 12:21).

But we have it made (Heb. 12:22 ff.). Not in the sense that we can relax, that we are *in.* We must still strive to enter—and it is a narrow door (Luke 13:24). We are still on the way—and since it is the way of *our* Lord, we are not content merely to eat and drink his real presence in our liturgy, not content merely to agree that he taught in Palestine's streets; we want to *follow* his way and hear and do what he taught us. We have it—made by Jesus Christ for us! He journeyed to Jerusalem for us (Luke 13:22; 9:51). He is the mediator of the New Covenant. His is the gracious shed blood sprinkled at the altar of the cross that has made our lives fit offerings to be poured out before the judge who is God of all (Heb. 11:24; Isa. 66:20; Heb. 11:23).

First Lesson: First, Last, and Always. "Some are last who will be first, and some are first who will be last" (Luke 13:30). If you are not in a hurry, willing to take a lower place in order to be moved up higher, that would not seem too hard to take. Just so we make it. But *last* may well mean *lost*. Will those who are lost be many? Isaiah testifies (66:15–17, 24). The Lord confirms (Luke 13:28).

If we would not be lost, we must put God first. And even before that must always be the loving action of God. He must come to gather all nations and tongues. He sent his Son as a sign among men. He has sent his disciples before his face declaring his glory. Their word must bring us as an offering to God. He must make us kings and priests before God, able to participate fully in the sacramental actions of the people of God.

We who for the most part were last, he has brought from East and West and North and South to sit at table in the kingdom of God (Luke 13:29). He who has risen up, the firstborn of many brethren (Rom. 8:29) has opened the shut door and no one can close it (Rev. 3:8). It is ours for always. "The kingdom ours remaineth." The new heaven and new earth which he has made are for always, says the Lord, and "Your name and your descendants shall remain." "All flesh shall come to worship before me," says the Lord.

And all who worship him, first and last, shall be with him always.

Second Lesson: Less or More? Who could ask for anything more? Why go back to anything less?

It would be less to think you had to do more. Those to whom this epistle was written were tempted to return to the old covenant, back to a relationship with God they understood as an "I will if you will." It seemed more sure if they could add up ceremonial observances and moral obediences and claim the total as the admission price. Then the only concern need be "How many?" (Luke 13:23) and not "Will *I*?" St. Paul used similar analogies from Mt. Sinai's thunder and lightning to urge those who would be saved by law to hear the law (Gal. 4:21–31). We cannot endure the order that was given (Heb. 12:20).

It would be less to think you had to do less. The God with whom we have to do (Heb. 4:13) is still a judge who is God of all (v. 23), and it is just men who are made perfect; it is those who strive who will live (Luke 13:24). Those whose confidence is in Father Abraham will have their premise confirmed when they see him and his sons in the kingdom, but they themselves will be thrust out (Luke 13:28). The Christian stress on *"mea culpa"* and *"miserere mei"* to be sincere must be augmented with what he who taught in our streets taught us to do for the street people (Luke 13:26).

Could there be more than to live in the city of the living God, the heavenly Jerusalem? Yes—to join in festal assembly with innumerable angels, and all the firstborn enrolled in heaven, and all those made perfect by God. More?—yes! To be with Jesus, God's son, to whom we were all Cains, but whose blood was able to atone and who is risen as our brother. More yet? Yes! To have it all now, even though not yet, for we have come! We have arrived!

Gospel: One Among Any. The proper question is not, "Will those saved be few?" but rather that asked by the disciples when our Lord said even the rich will find heaven's gate a needle's eye and their bulk of burdens like a camel. "How then can any?" And then the gloriously improper answer, "With God it is possible," possible even that I can be one among any (Matt. 19:23–26).

Possible, but not easy. Not merely a matter of beginning at the last moment to stand at the door and knock and say, "Lord, open to us." Not merely a matter of claiming, "You let our fathers in. We are of the same denomination." Not merely a matter of head knowledge, "We know who you are, Jesus who taught in our streets—you were conceived of the Holy Ghost and born of the Virgin Mary." No, not even, "suffered under Pontius Pilate, crucified, dead, and buried." "We know you" is not the password. Jesus' words pass us in—"I know who *you* are. I know where *you* come from! You have been conceived by the Holy Ghost in holy baptism and are among the firstborn enrolled in heaven (Heb. 12:23). You have believed and come to know that I am the Christ, the Son of the living God (John 6:69). You know that I was put to death in the flesh but made alive in the Spirit (1 Pet. 3:18), raised again for your justification (Rom. 4:25). Even though you, too, were workers of iniquity, you did not say, 'Be it far from you, O Lord' with Simon, nor with him follow afar (Matt. 16:22; 26:58 KJV), but you followed me on the way to Jerusalem and the cross (Luke 13:22). I know who you are. You are sprinkled with my blood, the mediating blood of the new covenant" (Heb. 12:24).

With God this is possible!

The Fifteenth Sunday after Pentecost

Lutheran	*Roman Catholic*	*Episcopal*	*Presbyterian and UCC*
Prov. 25:6–22	Sir. 3:19–21, 30–31	Eccles. 3:17–18, 20, 28–29	Prov. 22:1–9
Rom. 12:14–21	Heb. 12:18–19, 22–24	Heb. 12:18–19, 22–24	Heb. 12:18–24
Luke 14:1, 7–14	Luke 14:1, 7–14	Luke 14:1, 7–14	Luke 14:1, 7–14

EXEGESIS

First Lesson: Prov. 25:6–22. The Book of Proverbs combines several proverb collections. One of these begins 25:1 with the editorial comment: "Also these are Solomonic proverbs which the men of Hezekiah, King of Judah [715–687 B.C.], compiled [or: edited]." This collection ends with chap. 29. The main collection of Solomonic proverbs is 10:1–22:16; the maxims of 25–29 were evidently for one reason or another not included with them. It is possible that they were originally shaped and transmitted in the Northern kingdom (922–722 B.C.) and, after its fall, incorporated into the Southern (Jerusalem based) wisdom traditions.

The fourteen proverbs in 25:6–22 are warnings (6–7, 8, 9–10), comparisons (11, 12, 13, 14, 18, 19, 20), injunctions (16, 17, 21–22) and a statement (15), grouped together mostly by catchword/motif association. The variety of form reflects the different manners of instruction, interpretation, application, and transmission employed by the wise men when they offered "counsel" (Jer. 18:18 attests that the wise man played a basic role in ancient Israelite society alongside the priest and prophet).

The proverb in vv. 6–7 is the last of four sayings (vv. 2–7) concerned with wise action of or in relation to the king; it calls for a realistic assessment of one's position (cf. Ecclus. 13:8–13; Luke 14:7–11). Vv. 8–10 deal with legal matters: go into legal proceedings not hastily, only after careful consideration of the merits of your case (v. 8) and keep the case carefully confined to your own affairs (vv. 9–10). Vv. 11–12 praise timely speech and constructive criticism. A reliable messenger is crucial in a time when, as was then the case, written communications are expensive and rare (v. 13; cf. Genesis 24 for an example story of a trustworthy messenger and negotiator). Humorously and engagingly formulated are the satires of vain boasts of generosity (v. 14) and of the eventual success of patient and gently persuasive manners (v. 15; cf. Luke 18:1–8). Vv. 16–17 castigate the foolishness of "hogging" in matters of food (v. 16) and in matters of neighborly relations (v. 17). The ninth commandment of the Decalogue (Exod. 20:16) appears in v. 18 as a proverbial comparison, and v. 19 stresses that there is little reliance on a disloyal person when

dire emergency strikes. Untimely merrymaking is tactless and helps no-
body (v. 20). The wisdom of not reciprocating evil with evil (cf. 20:22;
24:29; Exod. 23:4–5; Matt. 5:43–47) is explained, underscored possibly
with a motif of an ancient Egyptian ritual that makes one's enemy repent
and give up enmity.

Like other peoples, ancient Israel probed the dimensions of social, cultural, and individual life and of society, seeking to surface orders thought
to be hidden there. Insights become manifest in striking, illuminating,
and memorable formulations as maxims, enabling the wise to offer counsel and all to live discerningly. ·

Second Lesson: Rom. 12:14–21. This letter, written by Paul in order
to introduce himself to the congregation in Rome whose help he needed
in his endeavor to preach in Spain (15:19–20, 23–24, 28), gives account of
the apostle's theology in order to reassure the Roman Christians and himself of their oneness in the gospel (15:32). Paul unfolds two systematic
courses of argument: (a) the thesis that God's righteousness, as manifest
in Jesus Christ, sets all God's creation—Jews and Gentiles alike—into the
reality of the new creation (1:18–8:39); and (b) the assurance that Israel's
rejection of Jesus is a mystery which will eventually be overcome by
God's faithfulness to his people (9:1–11:36). This is followed by several
parenetic sections (12:1–15:21) in which, either generally (12:1–8; 13:
8–10; 15:7–21) or with reference to specific issues, the indicative (the
reality) of God's new creation is shown to actualize itself.

The hortatory sayings in 12:9–21 are not systematically developed;
they are grouped by catchword/motif association on the basis of traditional parenetic material (not unlike Prov. 25:6–22). Several hortatory
motifs and formulations are known from intertestamental writings; many
allude to or quote OT passages. The two catchword/motifs are "love"
(12:9, 10, 13; 13:8–10) and "the good—the evil" (12:2, 17, 21). "Love"
as the most central term is the concretization (or actualization) of righteousness which, true to its OT understanding, is basically "covenantal
mutuality and loyalty" (but not an abstract idea or code of "justice").
Vv. 14, 17–21 have non-Christians in mind who are not to be shunned
and rejected when they oppose Christians (possibly formulated in contrast to the practice attested in contemporary Jewish groups where
occasionally non-Jews who opposed Judaism were liturgically excommunicated; cf. also John 16:2). Instead, Christians seek to commend
themselves to all by seeking peace and by doing good before (or: to?)
all men (vv. 17–18). The two OT quotations take vengeance out of man's
hands (vv. 19–20) and so bring "the good" to victory over "the evil"
(v. 21).

Vv. 15–16 deal with the relation of a Christian to his fellow Christians. Here God's righteousness is manifest as covenantal loyalty to each other: the person set free in Christ is flexible; "Christian freedom is freedom from all human conventions and norms of value" (R. Bultmann, *Theology of the New Testament,* Vol. 1 [New York: Scribner's, 1951], p. 343). Christians relate to each other functionally, like members of a body (12: 3–8) and hence will not set one or the other above the rest. Concretely, v. 16 refers to Christians who thought themselves to be more "spiritual" or "pneumatic" (1 Cor. 4:10; 10:25; 2 Cor. 11:19 also refer to such); they are exhorted not to think of themselves more highly than they ought.

True to the OT understanding of (God's, Israel's or man's) righteousness, the righteousness of the new human being in Christ is the flexible stance of Christlike covenantal mutuality and loyalty.

Gospel: Luke 14:1, 7–14. (For the general context of this passage, see the introductory remarks on the Gospel for Pentecost 13.)

Luke 14:1 shows Jesus sharing in a Sabbath meal at the home of a Jewish religious leader. There the Master, after healing a man with dropsy (vv. 2–6) and by way of table talk, warns against (Luke says: tells parables about) a thinking and acting that forces relations with fellow Christians into hierarchic patterns governed by prestige and into self-serving generosity.

Those invited were most concerned, Jesus observes, with the way in which their seating visibly indicated their superiority to others. As contemporary Jews already knew, such concern is vain since God speaks the last word. In fact, he has already spoken it: the now extended invitation to his (messianic) banquet goes to Gentiles and outcasts (cf. Matt. 22:1–10; Luke 14:15–24). Luke shifts this emphasis to that of ordering communal gatherings of the early Christians (eucharists?) in such a way that they reflect here and now the manner in which the coming messianic feast and age (for Luke: in the present period of the Holy Spirit) turns everything upside down (Luke 1:51–53): the one who exalts himself will find himself humbled (14:11; a saying which had been transmitted alone and illustrated in various ways: Luke 18:14*b*/9–14*a*; Matt. 23:12/1–11; cf. 18:4). In the light of 1 Cor. 12:12–30 one must ask whether *this* Lucan exhortation really overcomes prestige-oriented thinking!

The exhortation in vv. 12–14 and Matt. 5:46–47/Luke 6:32–35 show how much early Christian groups were tempted to withdraw into closed and self-serving communities. The motivation given in v. 14, however, is based on a rationale of (apocalyptic) retribution and so does not really overcome the sort of thinking castigated. Notable is the inclusion (in the kingdom) of the poor, the crippled, the lame, and the blind, probably in contrast to certain exclusive practices elsewhere (in Jewish and Jewish-Christian circles? cf. 2 Sam. 5:8 and certain rules of the Dead Sea covenanters; contrast Luke 4:16–22/Isa. 61:1–2).

These texts highlight Luke's interpretation of the gospel of the kingdom (no Synoptic parallels) in primarily ethical terms: it governs the Christians individually and corporately in the present period of the Holy Spirit when the certainty of the judgment (not its date!) is crucial.

HOMILETICAL INTERPRETATION

A theme for the day is *Living Beyond Existence*. The "will be" of the Gospel takes us beyond present existence: "Whoever exalts himself *will be* humbled and whoever humbles himself *will be* exalted—every one." These words of the Lord are not demonstrably true in our present existence. There is evidence of some, even of many, whose self-exaltation ended in a humiliation; but to human observation the odds against it are large enough that the majority of humanity lives the gamble. The "will *be*" indicates a force beyond the human factors and a time beyond present history. Whoever would live this kind of life must live by faith, in God, and in a God who rewards, and in a resurrection which provides a sequel to this life. He lives beyond existence.

Coexistence is an obvious necessity for the Christian though he might desire to "depart" as something "far better" (Phil. 1:23). The day's lessons spell out the pattern for inter-Christian relations (Rom. 12:16, etc.) and for relations with non-Christians (Rom. 12:14, 18–21; Luke 14:7–14; Prov. 25:6 ff.). Some of these attitudes and actions are possible simply as a philosophy of life—but "so far as it depends on you," and "if possible" (Rom. 12:18) indicate how "foes without and the foe within" can make it impossible. Jesus' pattern of living allows his disciples no alternative but to strive even then to make the impossible as possible as can be.

Beyond existence is the Christian's goal and his strength for living. Those who are impossible to live with he leaves to God (Rom. 12:19; Luke 14:11) and the possibility for Christian living he receives from God who has involved himself in our lives. A future blessing (Prov. 25:22; Luke 14:14) is something of an incentive, but the Messiah who blesses is the only initiator. All of this is said in relation to the kingdom (Luke 13:18–21; 14:15). God in Christ has not only said to us, "Friend, go up higher," but in Christ Jesus he has already raised us to heavenly places (Eph. 2:4–6). We are even now risen with Christ who gave his life for us and by his strength we can seek to do even those things that are above and beyond our human existence.

First Lesson: Sense and Non-Sense. The OT lesson, usually selected in reference to the Gospel, here also has a direct connection to the Second Lesson. These passages might be highlighted, or other of the injunctions pertinent to the parish life might be selected for application, those "offering counsel." But "to enable the wise to live discerningly" some clue is needed to make proclamation of the gospel possible.

The admonitions and warnings make sense, but our reluctance to act as sensibly as they direct is evidence of our need for the new mind and new heart which Jesus Christ came to give to men.

The non-sense is that which is folly and a stumbling block to those not called (1 Cor. 1:22–24). It is the gospel—Jesus Christ lived and died that the reward which God wants to give might be by faith, not by works, which no man has enough to boast of. It is the good news that Jesus Christ has been put to death, the righteous for the unrighteous (1 Pet. 3:18), so that in him we might become the righteousness of God (2 Cor. 5:21). These are the just—these who live by faith. These are accounted worthy to attain the resurrection (Luke 20:35).

Second Lesson: Offensive Humility. At the World University Games in Moscow, the United States basketball team led the Cubans 98–76 with ninety seconds to play. A scuffle for the ball threw players to the floor and suddenly the whole Cuban team ran on to the court swinging fists and folding chairs. The *International Herald Tribune* reported that a player from Providence College appeared to be the only United States player "who escaped unscathed. He climbed over a barricade around the court and sat down among the spectators" (I.H.T., 23 Aug. 1973).

Christians are not to live as spectators—neither are they to come out swinging. They are to be aggressively humble (Luke 14:11). The text spells out standards for life with fellow Christians (12:15–16) and for living with non-Christians and even persecutors (12:14, 17–21). (Standards for inter-Christian arguments are to be found in Matthew 18.)

"So far as it depends upon you" is as extensive as "seventy times seven." The Gospel for the day excludes friends, brothers, and kinsmen from the Christian guest list and opens it to the maimed, the lame, and the blind, all those who cannot repay (Luke 14:12–14). This text extends the dimensions of Christian concern to persecutors and enemies. And always the intention is offensive—that evil be overcome by good.

Jesus came doing good. But if his objective were *only* to give us an example "that we should do as he has done" (John 13:15) we would of all men be most miserable. What is worse than seeing another achieve what we are unable to do? He was good incarnate, good God incarnate, and overcame evil. By his life that even in death left vengeance to God, he absorbed our curses, our hard heartedness, our haughtiness and quarrelsomeness, our ignobility and vengeful acts. All this in our baptism has been buried with Christ. From that sepulcher none can roll away the stone. But even as he is risen from the grave, we are raised to newness of life. Risen, exalted, Jesus Christ was still their humble master. But no spectator he. He moved in on Peter: "Lovest thou me?" And even now, though our faces blush with shameful failure, we, his too-oft enemies, experience his coals of fire. He feeds us, he gives us to drink, his body and his blood in humble forms. And by his offensive he overcomes our evil with good.

Gospel: Live It Down. We are already "the more eminent man." We have been told by the host, "Friend, go up higher." We have been exalted. Now the trick is "to live it down."

God in Christ has given a great feast for us who could not repay. Even more—he has forgiven our prodigal past, put a robe on our shoulders and the ring of sonship on our finger. Now we are "to live it down."

We are to sit in the lowest place *every chance we get* in the marriage feast of the kingdom. *From where we are* we are to humble ourselves. But we are much more inclined "to live it up." We view our position as something the blessing of God has given us to enjoy—this papacy, or this profession as a doctor, or this cultural stance, or this white supremacy, or this inherited fortune, or these hard earned savings, or this orthodox doctrinal understanding. And all of us who are friends or brothers or kinsmen in any of these positions encourage one another in the conviction that since we have been exalted, we are now justified in living it up. If we have done wrong in all this we can never live it down. We need the converting power of Jesus Christ who humbled himself even to the death of the cross, and whom God has exalted. This mind is to be in us, and it is the mind *we now have* in Christ Jesus (Phil. 2:5).

It is well that we be challenged by this text. What have we paid out lately that we can anticipate being repaid at the resurrection of the just? Are we really trying to get on the second team, to help others get ahead? The Pharisees were watching Jesus and he taught them this lesson. If we keep our eyes on him, we too may learn.

The Sixteenth Sunday after Pentecost

Lutheran	*Roman Catholic*	*Episcopal*	*Presbyterian and UCC*
Prov. 9:8–12	Sap. 9:13–19	Wisd. 9:13–18	Prov. 9:8–12
Philem. 1, 7–17	Philem. 9b–10, 12–17	Philem. 7–17	Philem. 8–17
Luke 14:25–33	Luke 14:25–33	Luke 14:25–33	Luke 14:25–33

EXEGESIS

First Lesson: Prov. 9:8–12 (7–12). Prov. 1:1–9:18, the work of the final editor of Proverbs, functions as prologue to the whole book. The opening thesis is: "The fear of the Lord is the basis of wisdom" (1:7a), reiterated at the end of the prologue (9:10). After the (second) discourse of personified wisdom (Proverbs 8) the prologue is concluded by the contrast of personified wisdom (9:1–6) with personified folly (9:13–18). 9:7–12, in itself not homogeneous, intervenes between the two sketches as comment (footnote-like) on 9:6. It was put here by the final editor (or a later glossator? Vv. 9–10 or 10–12 are missing in some Hebrew manuscripts) because of the emphasis of the prologue (9:10); 9:11 is intended to continue 9:6 (or does it fit after 8:17?).

The appealing invitation of Lady Wisdom (9:1–6, 11), contrasted with the sweet yet deceptive attractions of Dame Folly (9:13–18), lays out the matter simply and clearly. There are two ways open: the one of virtue, the other of vice, the one leading to life, the other to death (4:18–19; Ps. 1:6; cf. Deut. 30:15–20; *Didache* 1–6). Yet experience shows that when it comes to grasping this fundamental issue, there are human beings whose minds are closed and whose critical faculty lacking while their mouths are open and their tongues unbridled. Such people are the subject of vv. 7–9, 12: a descriptive statement (v. 7) is followed by a prohibition (v. 8) and a command (v. 9), parallel to each other in that one formulates negatively, the other positively the recommended attitude; this is summed up by another statement formulated in two parallel conditional clauses (v. 12). The Hebrew word used to describe such people is rare in the OT; Prov. 20:1 compares them to wine in its seductive quality; 22:10 affirms that once they are expelled, strife, dispute, and abuse cease; 14:6, 19:25, and 21:11 show that they lack discernment; and 21:24 suggests that they are haughty and arrogant. They are, so our sobering footnote asserts, lost to the endeavors of the wisdom teacher as they take on more and more the character of wicked people. Hence, let the wise teacher concentrate his efforts realistically on those who listen and profit.

Prov. 1:7, the keynote for the final editor, is repeated in 9:10, to sum up the introduction to this edition of the inherited wisdom lore of old. It marks the early postexilic subordination of the more rationally and universalistically oriented traditions of the earlier wisdom schools, to the piety of the emerging synagogue, based on the law as sum total of the expression of the Lord's will for Israel, his people. We observe "a shift of emphasis from education to piety, from submission to the discipline imposed by a wisdom teacher to reverence for Yahweh. . . . 'Insight' is no longer intellectual clarity and discrimination, but religious illumination" (William McKane, *Proverbs* [Philadelphia: Westminster, 1970], p. 368).

Second Lesson: Philem. 1, 7–17. Paul wrote the letter to Philemon in order to straighten out an awkward situation: Onesimus, a slave of a leading Colossian Christian named Philemon and well known to (possibly converted through) Paul, had run away after (or: thus) doing damage to his master (v. 18). The escaped slave had made his way to Rome, the capital, which more than any other city attracted fugitives seeking anonymity. There he found entry into the Christian congregation whose outlook toward outcasts he knew from the house church of his master Philemon. Through (the imprisoned) Paul he became Christian (v. 10). As a new creature in Christ he was persuaded to "remain in the state in which he was called"; as slave, however, he was free to seek manumission (freedom) if the opportunity offered itself (1 Cor. 7:20–24). Furthermore, the fact that Paul, Onesimus' "father in Christ," was a fellow worker of his erstwhile owner, demanded that the situation be squared away and not be left to itself.

The letter, opening with the typical Pauline greeting formula (vv. 1–3) and thanksgiving (vv. 4–7), and concluding with greetings (vv. 23–25), sets forth Paul's tactful and deft handling of the matter: Onesimus returns to his master seeking reconciliation, supplied with a letter of recommendation which Philemon is persuaded (not commanded! cf. 8, 14) by the apostle to accept and act upon, especially since Paul formally accepts responsibility for any hurt inflicted or financial obligation incurred by Onesimus (vv. 18–19). Paul indirectly asks Philemon to give Onesimus to him as a permanent gift (vv. 13, 19–21) so that he may continue to be the apostle's assistant; evidently the request was fulfilled (Col. 4:9).

The passage contains most of Paul's carefully and somewhat humorously phrased plea for a reconciliation between the slave and his owner who had legal rights to mete out severe punishment. The apostle does not advocate the elimination of slavery, a feature of the prevailing social structure, from the Christian congregations. He is arguing neither for violent overthrow nor the unquestioning acceptance of the values and structures of society. While for the time being those who are slaves live *as though* they were not slaves (cf. 1 Cor. 7:29–31), Paul's principle as set forth in v. 16 would gradually and in the course of time soften the harshness of slavery and in the long run overcome it. The new life in Christ, at any rate, manifests itself without delay in the humanizing of human relationships; the escaped, rather useless slave is received back by his master not with the whip but as "hyper-slave," indeed, "as beloved brother" (v. 16).

Gospel: Luke 14:25–33. (For the general context of this passage, see the introductory remarks on the Gospel for Pentecost 13.)

Here as elsewhere in Luke, the fact that Jesus is followed by a crowd underscores the universal appeal and validity of the Master's words (cf. 5:1; 7:11; 11:27; 20:1). While Jesus is on a journey that leads him into further and further separation from the natural bonds of family and people, he turns around to spell out the conditions of discipleship. All are invited, even from the hedges and fences (cf. the preceding parable, 14:15–24), yet must consider their acceptance as a matter to be pondered carefully. The unit was composed by the evangelist; vv. 26–27 are probably from Q (cf. Matt. 10:37–38, also Mark 10:29–30 par.), while the twin parables of the farmer planning to build a tower (in his vineyard, cf. Isa. 5:2) and of the king faced by a stronger king came from the Lucan source. V. 33 is the evangelist's epilogue.

"To hate one's father . . . , even oneself . . ." (v. 26) does not have the primarily emotional and negative overtones we associate with the word (cf. the formulation in Matt. 10:37: "He who loves father . . . more than me . . ."). It means, rather, to put second, not to let somebody or something be one's first and only concern (cf. Deut. 21:15–17). "To carry one's own cross" (v. 27) is, as the use of the reflexive-possessive pronoun indicates, not the cross as symbol of martyrdom but the disciple's readiness to accept the daily adversity of being committed to his Master's cause; rabbinic and Stoic assertions similar to it are known.

The two parables (vv. 28–32), one from the humble world of the Palestinian farmer and husbandman, the other from the larger world of royalty and international politics, are offered by Luke as illustrations of the preceding words. They interpret the "either-or" of the disciple's total life as the *carefully considered* readiness for this kind of commitment. Luke 9:57–62 illustrates the point. Equally instructive is the (Lucan) parable of the good Samaritan: he in fact—though not in words—put obedience to God's will as known to him through the law first and thus above the excommunication which threatened him from his Samaritan kin.

For the evangelist Luke, Christian life as discipleship in the period of
the Holy Spirit is not a spontaneous response to a sudden stimulus nor
an eagerly reached-for soothing of a troubled mind nor a smug falling-in
with what is respectable.

HOMILETICAL INTERPRETATION

A theme for the day is *The Force to Face the Facts*. Our Lord spells
out very clearly what is required of a disciple (Luke 14:26–27, 30). We
are to renounce all for Christ. St. Paul is "bold enough in Christ to command us to do what is required" (Philemon 7); but he prefers to appeal
"for love's sake."

The first is a fact.

The second is the force.

"The fear of the Lord is the beginning of wisdom" (Prov. 9:10). The
wise man is he who hears and does what the Lord's word spells out
(Matt. 7:24). But the insight that enables us to appropriate the strength
of love comes from knowledge of the Holy One (Prov. 9:10). In this we
know love, not that we loved God but that he loved us and gave himself
for us (1 John 4:10).

It is clear that "hate" is not to be the emotion which rejects but is to
express the great priority we give to him whom we accept as God and
Lord. He does not want us to hate our life but with him to value it so
highly that we devote it completely to his service. However, we dare not
by such explanation rule out the total demand Christ places upon his
disciples.

The facts can be met, however, only by the force which God, the Holy
One, supplies. The preacher must share again "all the good that is ours in
Christ" (Philemon 6). The Gospel begins, literally, "As many crowds were
journeying with him" (Luke 14:25)—and that journey is to the cross. "If
any one comes. to me . . ." (v. 26), spoken by him whose face is set
steadfastly to go to Jerusalem, clearly includes the love that says, "Him
who comes to me I will not cast out" (John 6:37). He renounced all that
he had (Phil. 2:7). He renounced family, endured the cross, and gave up
his life out of love for us. For his love's sake he appeals!

First Lesson: The Word to the Wise. "Not many wise," St. Paul
says in another context (1 Cor. 1:26). Conditions of discipleship which
Jesus lays down in the day's Gospel would seem to support that in terms
of *this* text. It is not the wisdom of the world, but of the word, that will
make men wise unto salvation.

"The fear of the Lord"—no mention is made in the account of the
creation of the *awe* with which sinless man must have regarded the holy

God. But after men sinned they were afraid and hid themselves (Gen. 3:10). Now the direction must be reversed—men need now to hear of the wrath of God against the sinner, to discover that God is to be feared (Matt. 10:28) before they come to the fear of God that is the beginning of wisdom. Nor will the preaching of the law make a man wise. "Reprove a scoffer and he will hate you" (v. 8). Law increases the trespass (Rom. 6:20). The mind set on the flesh is hostile to God (Rom. 8:7). Man cannot stand a good God and does not care to know him.

But "the knowledge of the Holy One" is essential if a man is to become wise unto salvation. And so in the sight of all men, Christ Jesus "was made man" that men might gain insight. He was without sin, his being and his doing a living rebuke to the wicked. And he did indeed incur injury (v. 7). He suffered, the just for the unjust. But whoever sees Jesus Christ, sees the Father (John 14:9), whom to know is to love, and to love is eternal life.

Give this word to wise men and they will be wiser still (v.9)!

Second Lesson: Willing to Love. He who loves God will love his brother also (1 John 4:20). We cannot choose our brothers in our human families, those born according to the flesh (John 3:6); nor can we be selective of the brothers in the church, those born of God and the Spirit (John 1:13). Philemon loved Paul; but now he must love Onesimus, his slave (v. 16). Moreover his slave who had been useless to him, had perhaps wronged him (vv. 11, 18). As Christians we *will* love. The Gospel makes clear we must (Luke 14:25–33), but St. Paul here argues we surely will want to (Philemon 14)! How can we want to do what we don't want to?

Goodness is never created by compulsion. Paul could have commanded Philemon to do the loving thing (v. 8); but if an obedient Philemon had given his slave freedom or permission to return to serve Paul, it would not have increased "goodness" in Philemon even though it might have seemed "good" to Onesimus. Goodness is created by goodness, love develops by loving.

It was no mere rabbi who commanded men to love him more than even father and mother (Luke 14:26). It was the love of God incarnate, loving men even to his death that men might make love a way of life. "We love because he first loved us" (1 John 4:19). It is his love that makes us willing to love.

It is also by our loving that our love increases. Such loving does not first require "liking." True *agape* is love extended without expecting reward and without a prior lovable quality. That love has been created in us by his love. Now by our loving we increase love in our hearts and in the hearts of the saints (vv. 6–7).

If at first we cannot love as we should can we perhaps love selfishly? Even trying to love helps us focus on becoming more willing to love.

Gospel: To Beat the Ban. (The radical demands of this text make possible direct application to parish challenges which ought to be met. The root of the matter might also be exposed by an indirect approach. A parish that is consistently paying the cost may be helped by a sermon that supplies the coin for continued payment, and one that is confronted by overwhelming odds may need to hear of the ally.)

This is really too much, this uncompromising demand, this ultimate ban by the Lord of love. Surely he will with the testing supply a way to escape so that we may be able to bear it.

Let them take "goods, fame, child and wife"—but not life. Job managed a deal like that (Job 2:6), but God spared not his own Son (Rom. 8:32)!

About cross bearing—let us say to Jesus, "God forbid, Lord! This shall never happen to you" (Matt. 16:22) and he may never guess we really mean, "This should never happen to me!" But he became obedient unto death, even the death of a cross (Phil. 2:8)!

Let us build a great *place*, not a tower, a broad paved way where a great crowd can gather and cheer him and all his faithful disciples who will stand beside him. But they brought him to the place called "The Pavement" and they cried out, "Crucify him!" (John 19:13, 15).

It is all too much—we are outnumbered! Shall we send an embassy, sue for peace? There is no discharge in this war (Eccles. 8:8). But there is an ally, so great that "those who are with us are more than those who are with them" (2 Kings 6:15; John 14:23).

To all who receive him, who believe on his name, he gives power to become children of God (cf. John 1:12).

The Seventeenth Sunday after Pentecost

Lutheran	*Roman Catholic*	*Episcopal*	*Presbyterian and UCC*
Exod. 32:7–14	Exod. 32:7–11, 13–14	Exod. 32:7–11, 13–14	Exod. 32:7–14
1 Tim. 1:12–17	1 Tim. 1:12–17	1 Tim. 1:12–17	1 Tim. 1:12–17
Luke 15:1–10	Luke 15:1–32	Luke 15:1–10	Luke 15:1–32

EXEGESIS

First Lesson: Exod. 32:7–14. Exod. 32:7–14 is part of the section 31:38–34:35 (EJ) which intervenes between the giving of the ordinances concerning the tabernacle (25:1–31:37 P) and their execution (35:1–40:38 P). When Moses does not come down from Mount Sinai soon enough, the Israelites fashion a golden calf to fill the gap which Moses' disappearance had created for them. Their action, however, did not go unpunished. Eventually, Israel received the Ten Commandments anew. Exod. 32:1–8, 15–24, 30–35 rehearses the details of Israel's apostasy and its results from a Northern, prophetic viewpoint (the Elohistic strand of the Pentateuch); 32:9–14 was attached to this section as an affirmation that Moses' intercession prevailed against the Lord's decision to destroy Israel.

Exod. 32:7–8 belongs to E and illustrates its condemnation of the calf (bull) images. According to 2 Kings 10:28–29 the overzealous Yahweh-worshiper Jehu (842–815 B.C.) still found acceptable the golden calves set up by Jeroboam I in Bethel and Dan as pedestals for the presence of the God of Israel; the function of these golden calves was not unlike that of the ark in the Jerusalem royal chapel (1 Kings 12:28–30). Yet a century later Hosea condemned the calf of Samaria (8:5–6)—expressing the same sentiment as that found in Exod. 32:7–8. The claim that these calves are Israel's God from Egypt (v. 8*b*) follows literally 1 Kings 12:28*b* even though the plural form makes sense only in 1 Kings!

Exod. 32:9–14 is Deuteronomistic (cf. Deut. 9:12–29). It extols the power of Moses' intercession and has him advance not fewer than four reasons why Israel is to be spared: (1) it is God's people, (2) it has been set free at great cost to God, (3) its destruction now would give the Egyptians cause to ridicule a God who saves a people only in order to kill it in the (Sinai) mountains, and (4) the oath which God swore to the patriarchs (Gen. 15:5). The number and character of the arguments reflect later Israel's surprise that it survived at all—not only that legendary first apostasy but many others as well. It attributed that survival to the intercessory power of Moses. As a result, Moses' portrait was heightened to such nobility and selflessness that he is pictured as passing the opportunity to become himself a great nation superseding, as it were, "Father Abraham" as *the* father (32:10) and preparing rather "to venture into the breach" (cf. Ezek. 13:5) on behalf of his people. This feature of the Moses tradition was much stressed in later Israel (Ps. 106:23). Exod. 32:9–14 itself is cultic in formulation; cf. 32:11*b* with Ps. 136:11–12 and 32:12*b* with Ps. 85:5; also generally Gen. 20:7 and Amos 7:1–3/4–6.

Israel continued to ponder the miracle of its survival after many a turn to its own way and folly; Exod. 32:9–14 illustrates the certainty of exilic circles that the Lord responded to the prophetic-mediatorial intercession of Moses when the people were at death's door.

Second Lesson: 1 Tim. 1:12–17. This passage is the central part of
1:3–20 which serves to introduce and undergird the various orders for
the church in 2:1–6:2. 1 Timothy, like the other pastoral epistles (2
Timothy, Titus), originated toward the end of the 1st century A.D. in
Christian congregations where the Pauline heritage was strong (Asia,
Achaia, Macedonia) yet needed to be affirmed against certain Judaizing-
Gnostic trends (similar to those being combatted in Col. 2:8–15; see
exegesis of Second Lesson, Pentecost 10). 1 Tim. 1:3–20 counters these
trends by warning against self-styled yet really ignorant "teachers of the
law" (vv. 3–11), by contrasting their "empty talk" with the reliable core
of the gospel entrusted to the apostle Paul (vv. 12–17), and finally by
committing this apostolic instruction to the apostle's "genuine child, Timothy" (1:2; cf. 1 Thess. 1:1; 2 Cor. 1:1; Acts 16:1–3) who is constrasted
with two erring Christians (vv. 18–20).

Paul's startling change from persecutor to apostle, reflected in his own
occasional remarks (e.g. 1 Cor. 15:9–10; Phil. 3:4–7) and theologically
interpreted by Luke (Acts 9:1–30 par.), has shaped this passage. It
stresses that Paul's conversion be acknowledged as *the* prototype of the
Gentile's coming to faith in Christ and, more importantly, that Paul's
unique and exclusive commission to be the apostle to the Gentiles (cf.
Gal. 1:16; 2:9) makes him the only legitimate authority for handing *that*
apostolic work to the next generation (18–19). The contrast of "before"
and "after" in relation to Paul's conversion is stylized as missionary
paradigm, not as biographical information (13–14, 16, cf. Eph. 2:11–13;
for "in ignorance" [13] cf. Luke 23:34). Similarly the heightened description of Paul's and his successor's apostolic authority, in contrast to the
spurious, ill-founded claims of certain teachers, is more official pro-
nouncement than theological argumentation. Where Paul concretely
argued with his opponents, the pastoral epistles assume the matter to be
settled and prohibit debate; contrast, for instance, Paul's extensive debate in 1 Cor. 15:35–53 with the self-confident prohibition in 1 Tim.
1:3–7.

V. 15 presents as summary and core of apostolic preaching, beyond
doubt reliable and hence worthy of credence (cf. 3:1; 4:9), the assertion:
"Christ Jesus came into the world to save sinners" (similarly Matt. 9:13;
Luke 19:10). This (by now quite) creedal phrase, the (basically Jewish)
doxology (17; 6:15–16), and the full, liturgical style of vv. 12–19*a* may
reflect an emerging Christian ordination rite (v. 18!).

Thus the writer puts down Judaizing-Gnostic trends within postapos-
tolic churches with the affirmation that the prototype of Christian faith
is once for all given and exclusively set forth and transmitted by those
authorized by the apostle Paul. "The emphasis upon tradition in the

Pastorals means that Paul is being established as the authority for the church" (M. Dibelius/H. Conzelmann, *The Pastoral Epistles* [Philadelphia: Fortress, 1972], p. 7).

Gospel: Luke 15:1–10. This passage is part of the Lucan cluster of three parables (15:4–32), directed to Pharisees and scripture scholars protesting Jesus' keeping company with excommunicated people. The parable cluster, in turn, is part of the unique Lucan composition 9:51–18:14 which draws mostly on Q and L (the Lucan source). Jesus, himself "on the way to Cross and Exaltation," sets forth both in his action and his teaching how Christians accept into their fellowship the downs and outs of society during the period of the church, initiated and sustained by the Holy Spirit (Acts 1:8; 2:1–13).

Vv. 1–3 are the Lucan introduction to the parable cluster. Luke presents the parables as Jesus' answer to a theologically motivated reproach. Some of Jesus' (and Luke's) contemporaries would say that God accepts the gross sinner and the tax collector, who are evidently unrepentant and hence religious outcasts, only after and on condition of their repentance; some early Jewish texts even speak of God's joy over the death of the godless (Tos. Sanh. 14:10)! This "correct" sequence is inverted by Jesus: he announces that God's salvation is present reality; the sinner's *response* is repentance and restitution (cf. Luke 19:1–10; Mark 2:15–17 par.). The evangelist also highlights the joy over the coming into community and life of whatever (Jew or Gentile) outcast (in his two epilogues, vv. 7, 10; there the expressions "in heaven" and "before the angels of God" avoid naming God directly, and the correspondence of events on earth and in heaven is asserted).

As Matt. 18:12–14 shows, the parable of the lost sheep was probably part of Q (note its different interpretation by the first evangelist: it illustrates the responsibility of Christian leaders not to let even the littlest member of the congregation perish). Luke draws some additional features into the parable: the shepherd carries the exhausted sheep on his shoulders and invites his fellows to celebrate with him. Luke also attaches the parable of the lost coin, a twin (vv. 8–9, from the Lucan source?), in the interest of balance and comprehensiveness (similarly 14:28–32): it deals with a poor woman in a humble hut while the first parable presents a fairly well-to-do man in the open and rugged mountain pastures. (The Arab shepherd boy who chanced upon the Dead Sea Scrolls when searching for a goat is an apt commentary on 15:4–6.)

These two parables, like the following one concerning the two sons (15:11–32), invite those who claim to be Jesus' and (in Luke's time) the church's opponents on theological grounds, to a new consideration of the

issue at stake between them. Does not a person's joy over finding what
was lost and sorely missed, plead for reading anew: "I have no desire
for anyone's death. This is the very word of the Lord God" (Ezek. 18:32;
cf. Isa. 55:6–7)?

HOMILETICAL INTERPRETATION

A theme for the day is *Have Mercy on Us*. Mercy for sin . . . that is
what it takes. The OT lesson pictures a very "human" God, not that
humans might discount this accusation but that the revelation might
bring us to self-accounting and show us to be without excuse (Rom.
1:20). Human jealousy is wrong for it claims more than a man deserves.
God's jealousy (Exod. 20:5) can only be righteous for he deserves all
man's love of heart and soul and strength and mind (Deut. 6:5; 30:6;
Luke 10:27). The worship of things golden, life dedicated to feasting
and playing, results in cancellation of the covenant—"Your people, not
mine" (Exod. 32:7), God says to Moses. Worse yet, the worship of false
gods brings the wrath that consumes (v. 10). Moses made it as mediator
for Israel; thank God one greater than Moses cries "Mercy!" for us.

Mercy for selfishness . . . that is what we need. The saved so easily
resent those who need saving (Luke 15:1–2). Jesus told the two Gospel
stories not to show up the Pharisees and scribes but to help them shape
up. And he came to our planet not to condemn the world, but that the
world through him might be saved (John 3:17). That is the way of the
Man and mercy. God wills our sanctification and our unselfishness. The
mercy of God gives the unselfish Son that we might have the mind of
Christ.

Mercy for servants . . . that is what we have. St. Paul knew the mercy
of God had appointed him for service (1 Tim. 1:12–13). He is the foremost one (v. 16) but is an example for the least of us, and we servants
to the least of his brethren.

First Lesson: The Two "I's" of God. "I will have mercy on whom I
have mercy" (Exod. 33:19; Rom. 9:15). "I will no more have pity on the
house of Israel, to forgive them at all" (Hos. 1:6).

What do we make of that? of a God who can say that? and in our last
hour of a God who can do that?

His wrath is against the stiff-necked (v. 9). "Is" is the word of stress.
This is a present tense law. We tend to argue about when a neck is really
stiff. We ought rather be serious about how hot burns his wrath (v. 10).

After the golden calf was complete and Aaron had built an altar before
it, he still insisted, "Tomorrow shall be a feast *to the Lord*" (v. 5). God

said it was a feast to a molten calf. And God said, "To hell with it." It needs be said that way, for we too try to alter our calves with our lips rather than repent and "render the calves of our lips" (Hos. 14:1–3 KJV).

"The mercy of the Lord is from everlasting to everlasting upon them that fear him" (Ps. 103:17 KJV). That is the gospel. But God does not merely blink an eye at golden calves. It took a mediator—Moses—for Israel. It required God's own Son for the world—and to do more than to ask. He had to put his neck under the yoke of the law and fulfill it for us. And he had to endure the curse of law, even death for us. He was blotted out of God's book (v. 32)—"My God, why hast thou forsaken me!"

We ought not lose sight of the fact that the eyes of God watch continually for results of his gospel. God kept Israel as his people, but Moses forced each man to choose—"Who is on the Lord's side?" (v. 26).

He waits even now for our "I!"

Second Lesson: Believe vs. Behave. Parents are often impatient with their children's failures to be "good," and so are pastors with their people and so are we all with ourselves. The solution that recommends itself as most efficient and most complimentary is to urge, "Stop doing *that* and start doing the other." It seems efficient because it strikes at the obvious evidence of failure. It is complimentary because its implicit premise is that "we could if we would." This text urges "the divine training that is in faith" (v. 4) whose aim is "Love that issues from a pure heart and a good conscience and sincere faith" (v. 5). It argues for the training the Master gives his sheep by "laying it on his shoulder" (Luke 15:5) rather than giving it the lash or the law of the tongue. Strength for behaving is given to the believing, and ministry is by mercy.

The way of the impatient legalist is contrasted with the perfect patience of Christ which changed Saul to Paul, and gave an example for all who believe in him for eternal life (v. 16).

Paul knew what he was talking about when he castigated "certain persons" who desired to be teachers of the law "without understanding either what they are saying or the things about which they make assertions" (1 Tim. 1:6–7, 13). He had been one of them. Most of us have a dreadful affinity with them. Our parents told us to be good boys and girls more frequently than they helped us to be children of the gospel. That was something we could understand. We had learned "good and evil" (Gen. 3:5) because we desired the evil and did it, and knew the good as what we had not done. But our ignorance and unbelief (v. 13) view the law as something which shows us what is to be done instead of acknowledging what it really shows us—that we are undone. This unlawful use of the law (v. 8) is still a trap that can catch children of God, Jesus people, worshipers in marble churches, and the many who "don't belong to any particular church."

What luck!—to find the coin that was lost! What mercy to be the bad penny made good. What a mystery the mercy of God that chooses to forgive what is done in ignorance and unbelief—and even deliberately in unbelief and in spite of better knowledge!

The saying is sure, and surely should be said again and again—"Christ Jesus came into the world to save sinners." It is worthy of full acceptance and we should fully accept it that "the grace of our Lord overflow for us with the faith and love that are in Christ Jesus" (v. 14).

Gospel: Mercy Works. What do you say to sinners in church? "How do you do?" and try to avoid the thorn-raveled wool and the wilderness appearance? More to the point: How do you *do* with sinners? Greet them, wish them well? Or go after them as lost, and lay them on your heart, rejoicing when they are found? If it is profitless to say, "Go in peace, be warmed and filled" without giving the things needed for the body (James 2:14–17), is it not under harsher judgment to say, "Come in! Be forgiven and saved," without doing the things needed to keep body and soul together in heaven and with the angels of God?

Jesus is the example of mercy at work (1 Tim. 1:15), and Paul the foremost example of his successful work of mercy. One cannot expect a found coin to gain interest in coin collecting, nor a found sheep to develop the shepherd instinct. But the Christian who rides the Shepherd's shoulder, who knows by experience that mercy works, surely he should be caught up in this foremost work of mercy. "This man receives sinners and eats with them"—what a joy in the church and in heaven before the angels of God if more and more it can be said about each one of us!

The Eighteenth Sunday after Pentecost

Lutheran	*Roman Catholic*	*Episcopal*	*Presbyterian and UCC*
Amos 8:4–7	Amos 8:4–7	Amos 8:4–7	Amos 8:4–7
1 Tim. 2:1–8	1 Tim. 2:1–8	1 Tim. 2:1–8	1 Tim. 2:1–8
Luke 16:1–13	Luke 16:1–13	Luke 16:10–13	Luke 16:1–13

EXEGESIS

First Lesson: Amos 8:4–7. The passage 8:4–14 intervenes between the fourth and the fifth vision (8:1–3 and 9:1–4); it was placed there in order to explain "the certain end of my people Israel" (8:2). It is the first in a series of (partly secondary) sayings on this topic (8:4–7[8], 9–10, 11–14). The five visions (7:1–3, 4–6, 7–9; 8:1–3; 9:1–4) reflect how the man Amos was brought eventually, after two successful intercessions, to the certainty that the people among whom he lived was under sentence of death. In the light of this certainty he discerns, in matters public and private, breakdowns which for his contemporaries are "business as usual" (cf. 5:21–27).

Amos 8:4–7 is a good example of a prophetic oracle: it is made up of the actual message uttered on behalf of the Lord (v. 7), preceded by the prophet's own explanatory statement or diatribe (vv. 4–6). Only the former is direct word of God; the other leads up to it and relates it to the situation of those addressed. Several phrases used in these verses occur elsewhere in words usually thought to have been spoken by Amos: 8:4*a* is also found in 2:7*a*, 8:6 in 2:6*b*, and 8:7*a* in 4:2*a* and 6:8*a*. Hence it is possible that vv. 4–7 were spoken by a disciple of Amos, unfolding motifs which the master's own words contained.

The four different ways in which integrity in business life was undermined are described by way of quoting the impatient shop talk of the grain merchants: they cannot wait for the Sabbath and New Moon (when business had to stop, cf. Neh. 13:15–22) to be over, so that they can take advantage of those who already, due to the progressive differentiation of society into haves and have nots (cf. Isa. 5:8–10), live at or below the poverty line. By making the bushel measure (2/3 U.S. bushel) smaller by denting it or putting something inside it (so that less grain is dispensed), and by making the shekel weight (approx. 2/5 of an ounce or 11.5 g.) heavier (so that more silver chunks are given in payment), by changing the balance points of the scales (in favor of the merchant), by exploiting the custom of enslaving a debtor who was unable to pay (Lev. 25:39–40; Deut. 15:12–18), and by selling third grade grain, possibly even the sweepings from the storage bin (v. 6*b*), these sharks made their kill. Ancient Israel and other peoples of the ancient Near East knew that the well being of society depends on the integrity of its members. The Babylonian hymn to Shamash, as sun god all-seeing and hence god of justice, condemns him "who handles the scales in falsehood." In the OT this universal obligation is illustrated in Prov. 11:1, 26; 16:11; 20:10, 23; Deut. 25:13–16; Lev. 19:35–36; Mic. 6:10–11; and Hos. 12:8. Amos had to refuse to be fellow traveler with the thoughtless, easy going majority and to confront them explicit.

Second Lesson: 1 Tim. 2:1–8. The passage is the beginning of the epistle's main section (2:1–6:2). In it are set forth various orders for a church that is in the process of consolidating itself within society and the world. The range of matters treated illustrates how fundamental order and office had become in these congregations. (For the general context of this passage, see the introductory remarks on the Second Lesson for Pentecost 17.)

1 Tim. 2:1–7 enjoins as a first priority that Christians intercede for all men (v. 1) and especially for those in political power (v. 2). This is in keeping with God's will for all mankind as set forth by the one mediator Jesus Christ (vv. 3–6) and through Paul's genuine apostleship to the Gentiles (v. 7). The custom to pray for the (Gentile) rulers was old and traditional in Judaism. Already Jeremiah had exhorted the exiles in Babylonia to work for the good of and pray on behalf of that country, since they depended on its welfare (29:7). Cyrus, king of Persia, had the Jerusalem temple rebuilt and supplied with what was necessary for the ritual "so that they may pray for the lives of the kings and his sons" (Ezra 6:10; cf. Bar. 1:10–11; 1 Macc. 7:33). Christian congregations in the Pauline tradition systematized, almost a generation later, Paul's aside in Rom. 13:1–7 (cf. Mark 12:17 par.) into the catechetical topic "good Christian citizenship" (cf. 1 Pet. 2:13–17; Titus 3:1–2; contrast the description of the dangers and agonies Paul had to overcome in 2 Cor. 11:23–33). "The widespread distribution of this complex of ideas marks the changeover from an eschatological worldview to an ecclesiastical form of existence within an expanding world that provided more room for a Christian life" (Dibelius/Conzelmann, *The Pastoral Epistles* [Philadelphia: Fortress, 1972], p. 37). Note the formulaic, liturgical-catechetical language in vv. 1, 5–6.

The main part of vv. 8–15 concerns prayer by women (vv. 9–15); it is mainly related to woman's subordinate, yet not altogether disenfranchised, position (contrast Gal. 3:28). 1 Tim. 2:8 enjoins men everywhere (Mal. 1:11!) to lift holy hands—the prayer gesture was to stand upright and to stretch out the hands, palms open to receive, as it were, God's blessings. Hands are "holy" when they are lifted "without anger," that is, when they are stretched out in prayer to God *after* a person wronged has forgiven the one who prays (Mark 11:25 par.); they are lifted "without doubt" when the person prays in the assurance of being heard.

Gospel: Luke 16:1–13. This passage is part of a Lucan cluster of two parables (1–8, 19–31), framing several sayings which interpret both (16:9–18). For Luke the central theme of 16:1–31 is set forth in v. 13 . which, in the face of the kingdom of God now preached and present (16:16), demands clear and unambiguous response to the God whose kingdom is present (17:21). 16:1–31 stands within the wider frame of

9:51–18:14, the unique Lucan composition which draws mostly on Q and L (the Lucan source). In it Jesus, himself "on the way to Cross and Exaltation," sets forth in word and action the "either-or" of discipleship for the period of the church, initiated and sustained by the gift of the Spirit (Acts 1:8; 2:1–13).

Luke 16:13 sets forth the "either-or" of discipleship. Among Palestinian Christians this word of Jesus (collected in Q, cf. Matt. 6:24) was transmitted. It stressed that following Jesus *and* continuing to secure oneself through possessions are irreconcilable. The evangelist uses the word as one of his compositional themes for 16:1–31 (similarly Matthew in the "Sermon on the Mount").

Vv. 10, 11–12, both without parallel in Mark and Matthew, interpret the parable of the unjust steward as a warning directed to Christian leaders, especially treasurers or deacons (for a description of their function around A.D. 100 see 1 Tim. 3:8–13): do not be like that steward (cf. Luke 19:17; Mark 4:19)!

V. 9 gives Luke's interpretation of the parable. For the evangelist, this word of Jesus explains why the steward's action in the parable is commended as astute: because by giving away one's excess property as alms (Luke 11:41; 12:33), one is received into the heavenly booths, that is, into the state of those eternally blessed and happy (16:23–26), in the hour of one's death (individualized eschatology!).

V. 8 is offered as Jesus' own interpretation of the parable as it was transmitted to Luke. It contrasts in apocalyptic fashion the sons of this world with "the sons of light." This phrase and image was fundamental for the self-understanding of intertestamental pious circles out of which broadly based lay groups such as the Pharisees and the early Palestinian Christians and more exclusive priestly sects such as the Qumran covenanters emerged (cf. Eph. 5:9; John 12:36).

The parable is possibly based on a scandal generally known and refers to large-scale farm operations. The reduction in debt is for the same amount *of money* in each case. The point of comparison is the quick and astute reaction of the steward which ensures for him survival—his one, overriding concern under the circumstances. In like manner those confronted by the coming of the kingdom need to respond quickly, astutely, and singlemindedly (cf. the similar parable of the pearl, Matt. 13:45–46).

HOMILETICAL INTERPRETATION

A theme for the day in *Interest in Money*. It was a gesture, that was all. Even fifty measures of oil left the debtor hopelessly in debt—a year's production of seventy-five olive trees; and eighty measures of wheat would require a year's harvest of fifty acres. And Palestine was not Kansas. But at least it was a gesture that was practical. How practical is lifting up holy hands, even hands unstained by wrath and wrong (1 Tim. 2:8)?

The record of the church deserves the critical comment, "The sons of this world are wiser in their own generation than the sons of light" (Luke 16:8). That could urge us to be wiser sons in this life of light, or wiser in our life in this generation of the world. For Christians into whose hands have been placed both the mammon of unrighteousness and the true riches, Christians who are divided among those who have little and those who have much, those who only keep books balancing what is another's and those who have "what is their own," a sermon could warn about the dangers of our interest in money just for now and stress that we ought to use our money for eternal interest. The accent of the sermon could show what Jesus' whole incarnation, life, and death made devastatingly clear, that the way we live here will never earn us a place in the everlasting habitations of the just. We who try to serve God and mammon will fail to do either service well. The solution is to accept the complete service of God's mediator and then to devote mammon in return to service of the Father God, and the brother man.

The poor we have with us always (Amos 8:4-7); but surely the Christian should not be part of any process of persons or of economic systems that proceed to "take them in." Pray without ceasing we should (1 Tim. 2:1-8); but surely the Christian should not let holy hands substitute for open hands that share his own and his world's wealth with the have-not nations and the poverty-trapped. A Christian should have a great interest in money and make his money a servant to his greater interest—to be rich toward God.

First Lesson: A Place with the Son. The Christian lives as wheat among tares, corn among thorns. The Lord's instruction not to uproot the weeds but to let them grow alongside until the harvest clarifies one aspect of the life of the Christian in the world. But a more complex problem is how to cooperate with the world in its struggle for a place in the sun without compromising the place of the Son.

The way of invective, the pronunciation of the law, is one route for the church. Like Amos she can berate those who take advantage of the poor. Surely she should do even more than that about those who are *in* the church and know all about cult and church year (v. 5) but who make even the brotherhood pay off for their personal gain. The word of law is the voice of God's own wrath who "will never forget any of their deeds" (v. 7).

But the way of involvement is even more her route. It is demanded by the human nature and human life and death of Jesus Christ. He gave himself totally for men and completely to God. He too quoted God over against the injustices perpetrated by the wealthy over against the poor. He did not himself advance any three-phase economic program or any five- or five-hundred-year-plan for improving the lot of the common man; but he loved with a love greater than any man, and he brought in the kingdom in which we should love as he loved. He gave his life "a ransom for all" (1 Tim. 2:6), and that gift of new life is reason enough for Paul to urge common prayer that men might know a life "quiet and peaceable."

If life is to be made livable, surely the partnership proposed by God is not that Christians pray and non-Christians act. Christians must be defenders of ecology and discoverers of new sources of energy; must campaign for the rescue of the cities, must work to feed the world's hungry, must labor for the legal defense of men accused, the revolution in the care of aged, the children, the prisoners. But in cooperating for all these humanitarian goals, they must never omit their superhuman duty ("a teacher of the Gentiles in faith and truth," 1 Tim. 2:7)—to work with God that men "may be saved and come to a knowledge of the truth" (1 Tim. 2:4). A Christian cannot be for Christ and against charity, cannot be "oft in prayer" and not be always in politics, cannot be in the universal brotherhood and tolerate apartheid. But neither can he see bettering the lot of the oppressed ("Sit down quickly and write fifty," Luke 16:6) as a solution to the desperate need of humanity. What he does for men will also be done for God that men may see and glorify the Father and find a place with his Son.

Second Lesson: Lift a Hand. "He wouldn't lift a hand to help"—it's all too familiar an attitude. St. Paul here urges that holy hands be lifted in prayer for all men. Many of us come under the condemnation that we *don't* lift our hands to help, and some of us could possibly be thinking, "Even if we did, it wouldn't help." But the epistle urges with no limitations that we give our fellowmen a hand by lifting holy hands in prayer.

The instructions deal with public services and in context specify the male role in those services (cf. vv. 9 ff.). Its message is applicable to all Christians in all times and at all places and could be preached to other goals; but it might well be focused on the opportunity given us in Sunday services to stand with the whole church as a mediator for men.

"If we do, will it help?" Begin there. For one thing, the text calmly states the result—"that we may lead quiet and peaceable lives." It will make a difference in the quality of life in our whole country—not alone for Christian citizens (so that they can do their religious thing without being bothered), but for all in every position, high or low.

More than that—God sees this as the kind of thing which is "good and acceptable" to him because it is part of his own intention and action for men. He lifted his hand to help. He *took* hands, first—"and was made man." Jesus Christ, God's Son, stepped into the long human funeral procession and "touched the bier" (Luke 7:14) that he might raise men to new life. His hands fashioned a whip of cords (John 2:14) which he wielded to maintain the temple as a house of prayer (Amos 8:4–7; John 2:16). By his hands he was suspended on the cross as he gave himself "a ransom for all" (v. 6). He is "the one mediator between God and men" (v. 5).

"When we do, will you help?" That is the pertinent, personal question. "God desires all men to be saved and to come to the knowledge of the truth" (v. 4). "All men"—it is underscored by Paul's appointment as "a teacher of the Gentiles in faith and truth" (v. 7). What God desires and his Son brought to fulfillment ("for all," v. 6), that remains mysteriously dependent to some degree on our prayers. Mysteriously—because God's mind is already made up; what remains to be changed is the mind of those who know not or reject "the truth." And none of them can call Jesus "Lord" but by the Holy Spirit.

Where *he* fits in in all this is not our most important problem. He expects those who have a "knowledge of the truth" to stand with him who is the way, the truth, and the life, on behalf of those who have not yet come to "faith and truth." We—the church—stand before God who desires all men to be saved and who has indeed saved all men, as mediators with the one Mediator.

If you "get nothing out of the service" would you yet take your place in the assembly of the people of God to lift your hands in "supplication, prayers, intercessions, and thanksgivings" for all men?

Lifting holy hands for all men is a vital first step in giving a hand to one or two.

Gospel: Justifying Our Accounts. One must be shrewd in handling money among the mammon generation of our world if he is going to get ahead. The Christian ought be at least as shrewd in his handling of the true riches if he wants to be in with God. But he is surely making a disastrous mistake if he thinks that his use of earthly money is not evidence of his divine stewardship. His relation to mammon is indicative of his relation to God. What is shrewdness among the sons of this world can be compared to what is prudent among the sons of light.

The prudent man will know he is in all this with others. God did not save him alone, but saved the whole world (1 Tim. 2:3–6) and does not expect him to live alone but to be a part of the life of every man (1 Tim. 2:1). This steward knew his future was tied in with the other servants of the master (v. 9).

The prudent man will be faithful. The added warning of v. 10 reminds us that the point of the parable is not to approve what the steward did wrong, but to applaud how rightly he did it. But we are to do rightly what is right. And we get our practice with "very little" so that we can be entrusted with much, with the true riches.

The prudent man will be a singular servant—serving God alone. He will not serve the system that centers in mammon, nor will he serve the self that is the cause of its "unrighteousness."

Most of all the prudent man will not try to justify himself. The Pharisees to whom Jesus addressed this parable "were lovers of money" and they scoffed at him. But he said to them "You are those who justify yourselves before men, but God knows your hearts" (Luke 16:14–15). Being outstanding man among men has no relation to good standing with God. Jesus came preaching the kingdom of God. That kingdom is entered violently. The violence Jesus suffered at the hands of men tore open the veil that blocked us from the kingdom. That violence has made it possible for us to tear ourselves away from mammon to serve the living God.

The Nineteenth Sunday after Pentecost

Lutheran	*Roman Catholic*	*Episcopal*	*Presbyterian and UCC*
Amos 6:1–7	Amos 6:1a, 4–7	Amos 6:1, 3–7	Amos 6:1, 4–7
1 Tim. 6:11–16	1 Tim. 6:11–16	1 Tim. 6:11–16	1 Tim. 6:11–16
Luke 16:19–31	Luke 16:19–31	Luke 16:19–31	Luke 16:19–31

EXEGESIS

First Lesson: Amos 6:1–7. Framed by the oracles against neighboring nations, Judah, and Israel (1:3–2:16), and the (expanded) series of the five visions (7:1–9:10[15]), chaps. 3–6 contain (later annotated) groups of words denouncing the corruption of society and religion in the Northern kingdom during the reign of Jeroboam II (c. 760 B.C.). One group is made up of two "woe" oracles (5:18–21 and 6:1–7). "Woe" was the opening exclamation of a funeral lament (1 Kings 13:30); prophets such as Amos used it to introduce and shape their message of imminent disaster, a message which sees the one addressed as virtually dead (cf. Amos 5:1–3).

The mention of "those at ease in Zion" is a Deuteronomistic application of the inherited word of Amos to the capital of the Southern kingdom. By this time (Babylonian exile) Jerusalem had to be seen as equally threatened by and eventually succumbing to the same fate as Samaria, capital of the Northern kingdom Israel until 721 B.C. V. 2 and part of v. 6 ("not caring about the ruin of Joseph") are actualizations of the word of Amos as it was alive a generation later among his disciples. In the wake of the conquests of Tiglat-Pileser III (745–727 B.C.), neighboring cities and states were overrun, not to mention the Northern kingdom's near defeats! Should this not teach the Samarian leadership class to read the signs of the times and be broken ("sick") over Joseph's (the Northern kingdom's) threatening ruin?

Amos, called to prophesy against the Northern kingdom (7:15), castigates the selfish, thoughtless, and gluttonous life of its leadership in the capital. Confident that they are superior to others, they give no thought to the normal and natural outcome of their behavior (cf. Prov. 11:28). Foolishly they ignore the maxim that "the day of disaster" (Prov. 16:4) will surely come. Instead they crassly use only the best and most luxurious: they own ivory-inlaid beds (excavations in Samaria have brought to light exquisite, probably Phoenician ivory carvings used for inlay or decoration) and couches on which to stretch out for feasting; they eat rams and calves which are tender and of the highest quality; they are entertained (or entertain themselves) with singing and music (cf. 1 Chron. 15:16; "like David" is probably a later annotation which came into the text, cf. 2 Chron. 29:27); they gulp wine out of mixing or serving dishes (instead of the smaller, more appropriate cups), and perfume themselves with choice oils (cf. Eccles. 9:8). As detailed as this unique description is, brief and pointed is the announcement (v. 7) of what will befall those "at the top," who indulge "in noisy feasts": they will march "at the top of the prisoners' column," and their "noise will give way" to the silence of those brought low.

Second Lesson: 1 Tim. 6:11–16. This passage is part of the concluding section of the epistle (6:3–21) which, like the opening section (1:3–20), sets the church orders given in 2:1–6:2 into the context of the trusted office for which the apostle had authorized the congregational leader of a new day. (For the general context of this passage, see the introductory remarks on the Second Lesson for Pentecost 17.)

1 Tim. 6:11–16, in contrast to the preceding and following exhorta-

tions, focuses on the obligations which were laid upon Timothy as office-holder. Allusions to a rite of initiation are evident, directly in v. 12 and indirectly in v. 11. V. 13 contains a two-part creedal formulation (God/ Christ, cf. 1 Cor. 8:6), and vv. 15–16 are of hymnic character. Hence Ernst Käsemann has suggested that the writer here is recapitulating certain aspects of the ordination of Timothy, in fact, that this is the earliest direct attestation of a Christian ordination rite; cf. 1 Tim. 1:18; 4:14; 2 Tim. 1:6; 2:2. This hortatory recapitulation is connected with the preceding warnings (6:3–10) by the phrase: "But you, man of God, flee these!"

The passage then moves on more generally to a list of obligations which are laid on the Christian who has become a new creature through baptism (vv. 11b–12a). The ordination vow, made publicly, is mentioned (v. 12b), followed by the command (v. 13a) to preserve the "deposit," (cf. 6:20) which ordination laid exclusively into the ordinand's hands, complete and unchanged until the (second) coming of Jesus Christ (v. 14). This command is buttressed by a theological aside; it uses an inherited creedal tradition to parallel Jesus' own public "witness" before Pontius Pilate with that of Timothy at the time of his ordination (v. 13b). The passage is completed with an elaborate doxology of God who in due time "will show" Jesus' appearance (vv. 15–16, possibly formulated in contrast to the titles of Oriental and Roman rulers; cf. Dan. 2:20–23).

Characteristic for the pastoral epistles is the combination of OT, Jewish-apocalyptic, Hellenistic, and Pauline motifs; cf. the coordination of "righteousness" and "faith" (Rom. 3:21–22) with the virtues of "patience" and "gentleness," the convergence of OT and Hellenistic connotations in the phrase "man of God" and both Jewish and Hellenistic motifs in the closing doxology. Like the evangelist Luke, the writer stresses the present time as the period when, in retrospect to the example of the suffering Jesus and in anticipation of the final coming of Christ, Christians and their leaders, apostolically legitimized, "fight the good fight" (2 Tim. 4:7; Phil. 3:12–14; Acts 20:24, 28–32).

Gospel: Luke 16:19–31. (For the general context of this passage, see the introductory remarks on the Gospel for Pentecost 18.)

The parable (vv. 19–26) is presented without introduction (except in the Western text, which has: "He told yet another parable") and application because for Luke it clinched two points which he presented in the sayings 16:14–15, 16–17. The parable itself is double-pronged: vv. 19–26, taking up 16:14–15, affirm that after death the condition of the feasting, thoughtless rich man and of the starving, diseased beggar will be inverted, while vv. 27–31, taking up 16:16–17, assert that a sign will not be given to validate miraculously the plain demand which "Moses and the prophets" (God's will as set forth in the OT) make concerning man's humanity to man (cf. the manner in which the Samaritan had "heard" that demand, 10:25–29 with 10:30–37). For the evangelist the example story underscores the assertion that in the hour of a person's death (note Luke's individualized eschatology) his or her clear and obedient response to God's will is decisive. Those who claim to be Abraham's children (16:24; cf. Matt. 3:7–10 and Luke 3:7–9) yet have ignored the corresponding obligation and will find themselves shut out from the heavenly banquet where "the true Israel" feasts with the patriarchs (cf. Matt. 8:11).

Various details of the realm beyond physical death, such as "underworld, paradise, and the chasm separating the two," "Abraham's bosom" (= sitting at his right, the place of honor, cf. John 13:23–25), refreshing water, are attested in Jewish-apocalyptic literature; cf. 4 Ezra (2 Esdras) 7:36. Interpreters point out that a similar story circulated among rabbis and, outside Palestine and earlier, in ancient Egypt. Jews from Alexandria probably brought it into Palestinian-Jewish lore. In this context (16:1–31) Luke employed it to support his typical warnings to the rich (6:20–26!); in the parable of the great supper (14:15–24) the motif of the rich man stands behind the figure of the well-to-do but snubbed host —a newly rich tax collector who in this fashion tried "to make it in society."

The exchange between the rich man and Abraham (vv. 27–31) across the unbridgeable chasm (v. 26) is a Lucan (or pre-Lucan?) rendering of Jesus' refusal to grant a sign (cf. Mark 8:11–13; Luke 11:16, 29–32). Seeking such an extraordinary validation of the plain demand of God is nothing but pretext for avoiding its claims! Already the Deuteronomic preachers knew this (30:11–14), and the evangelist John unfolded it in his way (11:1–53). The phrase "Moses and the prophets" refers to the two, by then canonical, collections of sacred writ: the law (Genesis–Deuteronomy) and the prophets (Joshua–2 Kings, Isaiah, Jeremiah, Ezekiel, and the twelve minor prophets). In Luke's theology the phrase attests these as the sufficient manifestation of God's will for Israel "until John" (16:16). "After John," when the kingdom is preached and present (16:17; 17:20–21), the law and the prophets remain in order to be "opened" by the risen Christ as those that attest him (16:17; 24:27).

HOMILETICAL INTERPRETATION

A theme for the day is *The Children's Obligations.* The rich man in Jesus' story knew something had gone terribly wrong. He pleaded, "Father Abraham, have mercy upon me . . ." According to the understanding of the Pharisees, riches were an indication that everything was going all right. God rewarded the good with goods. But here he was in Hades, and the beggar Lazarus, whose misery in life should have been indication of some failure before God, was at Abraham's feast, reclining on a couch in the place of honor very close to the host. Luke had quoted John the Baptist's words early in his Gospel, "Do not begin to say to yourselves, 'We have Abraham as our father' " (3:8), and here he records the story Jesus used to reinforce that point. But if the lesson is to be for us, we might consider how frequently we call God, "Father" and how we repeat, "have mercy on us." John's words and Jesus' lesson should be for us: "Bear fruits that befit repentance." All the signs that God has given have been given, and we now have "Moses and the prophets." We had best hear them and be clear on our obligations as children of the heavenly Father.

The prophet Amos speaks to us today: "Grieve over the ruin of Joseph" (Amos 6:6). Our grief will not be for the Northern kingdom, but we ought to see in the poor all around us in our land and our world the ruin of humanity as evidenced in its inhumanity. For most of us the question of obligation is a matter of degree—but so was it for the rich man. He permitted Lazarus to beg at his gate. He fed him what fell from his table. Are our scraps of charity actually the fulfilling of the children's obligations? Grieve!

The epistle sets positive exhortation between two passages dealing with the negative power of riches (1 Tim. 6:10 and 17–19). We are to "take hold of the eternal life to which we were called" (v. 12). And our "riches in good deeds" lay up "a good foundation for the future so that we may take hold of the life which is life indeed" (v. 18). These are wide circles on the target—"righteousness, godliness, faith, love, steadfastness, gentleness"; but surely our aim will not be to land somewhere in the general vicinity. We would aim for these as the center of "life indeed!"

Phrase our obligations in terms of the latest campaign advertising of the community chest. Then read the appeal of the epistle: "O man of God!" Jesus Christ, who summed up his entire life's purpose before Pilate in his kingly silence and his servant's death has made us men of God, children of the Father. Do we think of obligations, or of opportunities?

First Lesson: Put It Off. It could be instructive to imagine Amos confronting our civilization (remembering that *we* are civilized people) and phrasing his denunciation in current terms. We who lie upon inner spring mattresses and stretch ourselves upon "perfect sleepers." Our per capita consumption of meat, our deep freezers that make certain of our supply, Muzak and radio and TV to supply us with "idle songs," bowls of Sea-

grams, and Brut for anointing . . . and add to this all the buildings and
appurtenances we employ to make ourselves "at ease in Zion" . . . and
the immense budget we contribute to that makes us "feel secure on the
mountain of national defense."

We too would "put far away the evil day"; we hope to outlast the day
of reckoning. It certainly is a complicated business—"What can *I* do about
it?" But we cannot put it off. We must deal with the necessity for revolution in our economic and social structures. What we undertake to do
now, we can hopefully accomplish without bloodshed. What we try to
put off "brings near the seat of violence."

If we are no longer to "put off," we must "put on"—"the new nature,
created after the likeness of God in true righteousness and holiness"
(Eph. 4:24; 1 Tim. 6:11). We cannot put that new nature on just by
being told to put it on, no more than the red dust shape that looked like
Adam could breathe into itself the breath of life and become a living
soul. It is the Christ, and him being condemned before Pontius Pilate,
crucified, dead and buried and him risen from the dead who must be
proclaimed to give anew this nature. Then we can "put on, as God's
chosen ones, holy and beloved, compassion, kindness, lowliness, meek-
ness, and patience" (Col. 3:12).

Second Lesson: The Changing of the Guard. "Keep the faith—if you
can identify it." A cynical departure line, but today often too true. How
different from St. Paul's injunction, "Fight the good fight of the faith"
(v. 12); "Keep the commandment unstained and free from reproach . . ."
(v. 14). The word "keep" means "to guard," and "the commandment"
sums up all that Jesus said to us and did for us.

He put these words together himself (John 14:15, 21; 15:10) and so
instructed his disciples.

After all his teaching of the kingdom, after showing that he had come
to lay down his life as a ransom for the sinful world, after his determined
journey to Jerusalem, he "witnessed" that it was indeed the truth that
this was the way that the world would have life from God. It was "a
good confession," a noble confession, that he made before Pontius Pilate,
noble of him and good for us. "He was crucified, died and was buried.
And the third day he rose again from the dead." When he returned to
his disciples after that "little while," he instructed them to make disciples
who were "to observe—to keep, to guard—all that he had commanded"
(Matt. 28:20).

There is here a kind of changing of the guard. He obediently "kept"
all that God commanded him. And now he passes on that responsibility
to guard to his disciples. He instructs them to teach disciples in all na-

tions to guard "the commandment." They have taught disciples and those disciples other disciples, until now we have the task to guard.

At this moment we can look at ourselves as at a single frame of a motion picture of the changing of the guard which has suddenly been stopped. It is like the childhood game of "pass it on" in which one person whispers a sentence to the person next him, who must pass it on, and so on around the circle. The last person then says what he has heard, and the point of the game is to see how much the final statement is like the first. Right now—we who have heard "the commandment" pause to consider what we have heard. We "guard" it, examine its truth, study it, practice proclaiming it, determining faithfully to pass it on.

At our baptism we were given life by the God who gives life to all things. We were called to take hold of life. We made the good confession before many witnesses ("The saints above and those beneath / But one communion make . . ."). Our charge is now to keep the commandment unstained until the appearing of our Lord. But it is also to "take hold" of the eternal life (vv. 12, 19), to wield it as a weapon for good, serving him whom no man has ever seen or can see through those we can see, especially the poor whom we have ever with us.

He alone has immortality. We do not have all the time in the world.

Gospel: Relating to the Father and the Son. The rich man calls Abraham, "Father," and Abraham calls the rich man, "Son." The rich man has five "brothers" but should have had six—the one he did not acknowledge was Lazarus. "Moses and the prophets" are somehow involved in the relationship, but the rich man does not think much of them. All of these reveal something about relating to God our Father.

Money does not establish the relationship. The Pharisees concluded that if a man were blessed with this world's goods it was a sign that he had a good relationship with God. But Jesus here makes a special point of showing that it is not so.

Poverty, however, does not establish the relationship either. Jesus is not setting up the means of salvation in describing a man without means. If we are wondering, we are not half as curious as the rich man!

He thinks that a miraculous sign would do it. If dead Lazarus would appear to his five brothers, that would jolt them into a relationship. But Abraham says, "No. If they do not hear Moses and the prophets, neither will they be convinced if someone should rise from the dead."

That leaves Moses and the prophets as the way we can be related to God. They were agreed that God was a God who loves and out of his love accepts, even sinners. And they were also agreed that a man who accepts God's love obviously will love those whom God accepts.

That is hard to believe. And equally difficult to do. Clearly this Jesus is a Son of the loving God, for he accepts us even when we fail. "Beginning with Moses and all the prophets, he interprets to us in all the scriptures the things concerning himself" (Luke 24:27). And for good measure, he rises from the dead!